DISCOVERING TECHNOLOGY

BOOK 1

COLIN LEVER

Causeway Press Ltd

In memory of my father, the late 'Jack' Lever

To the teacher

How this book is organised.

Chapters 1-6 show exactly how to design and make things using design and technology as a process. The chapters clearly explain how to identify needs and opportunities, generate design ideas, plan and make designs and evaluate what has been made.

Chapters 7-13 contain all the skills needed when designing and making. The chapters can be used in any order. They can also be used in conjunction with chapters 1-6. For example, organisational skills are important when researching, designing, making and evaluating.

Chapters are divided into half page, single page or double page spreads. Each contains one or more activities. Activities develop design and practical skills. Some activities are based on information in the book. Others encourage students to try things for themselves.

A Teachers' Guide is available. It is photocopiable and contains advice for teaching, guidance on marking and assessment, and suggestions for practical skills work.

To the student

Some people think Technology is about machines. This series of books shows you that Technology is much, much more. Technology is about designing and making. You will work with food, fabrics, wood, paint and other materials. You will design many different things (some of them on machines!). You will learn to improve and change your designs so that people can really use them.

The activities have been written with your needs in mind. You will be encouraged to think for yourself, solve problems, invent and be creative. You will find the activities challenging and stimulating. There will be opportunities to design and make things for use at home, at school, in business, in recreation and in the community.

Enjoy your discovery of Technology. Who knows, you may be the next great inventor, businessperson or designer!

Contents

Acknowledgements

Cover and page design Andrew Allen
Cover drawing Steven Hunt provided by The Image Bank
Typing Ingrid Hamer
Photography Ian McAnulty, Andrew Allen
School photographs Heywood Community School, Rochdale and William Temple High School, Preston
Illustrations Alan Fraser
Graphics Caroline Waring-Collins

The author wishes to thank the following for help and contributions toward the writing of this book

Bruce Mager, Head of Technology, Matthew Moss High School, Rochdale

Pauline Ferguson, T.V.E.I. Co-ordinator, Hollingworth High, Rochdale

Angela Thompson, Head of Technology, Wordle High School, Rochdale

Stephen Blockley, Rochdale T.V.E.I.

Linda Renney, Head of I.T., Hollingworth High, Rochdale

Ian McAnulty, Head of Creative and Performing Arts, Heywood Community School, Rochdale

All staff and students at Heywood Community School, Rochdale

Rochdale L.E.A.

Rochdale T.V.E.I.

Elaine Lever

Matthew Lever

Aidan Lever

Picture sources

Eye Ubiquitous p.13 (worker), p.50; Sally and Richard Greenhill p.36 (dig), p.40 (shoes), p.42 (traffic); Popperfoto p.88 (models); Stuart Rutter/Harte Rutter p.87, p.94 (chair); Sefton Picture Library p.15 (spaceman), P.17 (bridges), p.28 (welder), p.91; Topham Picture Source p.12, p.15 (old kitchen), P.27 (athletes), p.36 (motor show); Travel Photo International p.4 (banquet), p.46 (boat).
The page on p.59 was reproduced with kind permission of BT Yellow Pages. Yellow Pages is a registered trademark of British Telecommunications plc in the UK.

Every effort has been made to locate the copyright holders of material in this book. Any omissions are regreted and will be credited in subsequent reprints.

Causeway Press Ltd
PO Box 13, Ormskirk, Lancs, L39 5HP
© Colin Lever 1992
1st Impression 1992

British Library Cataloguing in Publication Data
Discovering Technology
   Book 1
   607.1041
   ISBN 0 946183 740

Typesetting by John A. Collins (Picatype), Ormskirk, Lancashire L39 1QR

Printed and bound by Butler and Tanner, Frome and London

What is design and technology?

Many of the things around us are designed and made. Why? Imagine that you need to carry fresh food home from the shops quickly. How will you do it?

You need to solve this problem. In design and technology we try to find solutions to **problems**. We create, adapt or change things to satisfy our **needs**. You might design some of the things across the page to help get the food home.

Activity

▶ Make a list of all the things that you might design and make to get fresh food home.

▶ Discuss what has been designed and made to meet the following needs:
 (a) to get a message to a friend
 (b) to keep a garden tidy
 (c) to find our way around a city
 (d) to stop litter
 (e) to record lists of names
 (f) to keep food cool.

Designs to help get fresh food home

In everyday life we see many things that are designed to satisfy people's needs.

Activity

▶ What needs are the designs in these photographs satisfying?

A computer

A water park

Padded and nylon jackets

A banquet

What will you design?

The things that you will design and make fall into three groups.

Artefacts - these are objects such as a chair or a piece of pottery. They do not usually have moving parts.

Systems - are objects or activities which work together to do a job. Cameras have electronic and mechanical systems which make them work. Your school might have a rota system for school meals.

Environments - your surroundings, such as your school or house. You might live in a safe environment at home because you have a burglar alarm.

Activity

▶ Use the information on this page to help you decide if the following are artefacts, systems or environments.
  (a) A skirt and a pair of trousers.
  (b) A mobile to hang in your bedroom.
  (c) The local park.
  (d) A set of traffic lights.
  (e) School meals.

Artefacts
Early people made stone tools. Today tools and equipment are made from metals and plastics.

Systems
Early people lifted heavy stones with wood and rope. Some people pushed and others pulled. Today cranes move objects using electronic and mechanical systems.

Environments
Early people lived in huts made from animal skins. Today we live in brick houses with many rooms. The houses are safe, clean, warm and dry.

Designing artefacts, systems and environments

Sometimes the things that you design and make can fall into more than one group. A computer is an artefact, but it is made up of an electronic system which makes it work.

Activity

▶ Look around your school library or local library.
Write down the things that you think are:
- artefacts
- systems
- environments.
Discuss your results with others.

▶ What parts of:
- a telephone box
- a local sports centre
are artefacts, systems and environments?

Your library has many artefacts, systems and environments

How will you decide what to design and make? Imagine that you and three of your friends are stranded on a desert island. The island already has fruit, some animals and drinking water when you arrive.

You have with you:
- food for two months
- matches
- knives
- a saw.

You will not be rescued for at least three months.

Activity

▶ What needs would you have to satisfy before you are rescued?

▶ Discuss the artefacts, systems and environments that you would design and make to survive on this desert island.

▶ Make a list of the things you would design and compare it to another group's list. How are the lists different?

Where do you find design and technology?

Look around your school and classroom. Look about you on your way home and in your house. Look around the shops and factories in your area.

You will see many designs in these different **situations** or **contexts**. Contexts can be any of the things in the diagram below.

Designs often fit into more than one context. You could design a colourful logo for your school or community centre, or for a business.

Activity

▶ Where would you find the following?
Remember that they can fit into more than one context or situation.
(a) An electric light.
(b) A smoke detector.
(c) Waste disposal.
(d) A creche to look after young children.
(e) An athletics meeting.

▶ Choose an artefact, system and an environment that you might find in your school.
In which other contexts would you find each of them?

At school

In business and industry

At home

Contexts

In the community

For recreation

How do you design?

When you design and make something you use the **design and technology process**. A process is a number of tasks that are linked together.

Let's design a microwave meal. The design process is like a **cycle**. You can start at any point and come back to it as many times as you want to.

You could start by doing one of these tasks first:
- find out if people need a microwave meal and the type they might need
- design a few meals and pick the best
- plan and make a microwave meal
- evaluate other microwave meals.

When you have finished the task, you carry on to the next task in the cycle. You can see the process for designing a microwave meal called Snackspots below.

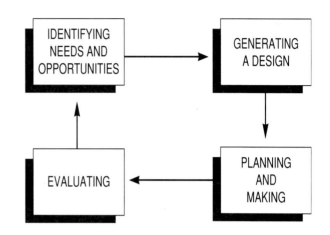

The design and technology process

Identifying needs and opportunities

Research and investigate if there is a need and opportunity to design and make a microwave meal.

You might think about:
- who needs it
- who will buy it
- what type of meal they want
- what packaging people will like
- if there are opportunities to make it
- what needs are satisfied.

Record and present your results.

Evaluating

Evaluate and test the microwave meal. Evaluate how it was made. Can it be improved?

You might think about:
- if the package is suitable
- if the meal is suitable
- if it costs too much
- if it is better than other products
- if it is made in the best way.

Record and present your results.

Activity

▶ Find a need for a new type of:
(a) shoe or
(b) biscuit.

Design:
(a) a hairstyle or
(b) a database for bus times.

Plan to make:
(a) an evening meal or
(b) a nature trail.

Evaluate:
(a) a wrist watch or
(b) any room in your house.

Discuss and write down the things you might think about when carrying out each task.

▶ Think of a design or choose one of those below.

Follow it through the whole design and technology process.

Write down the things that you might think about at each stage.

(a) School uniform.
(b) A clothes line.
(c) A way to lose weight.
(d) A design to keep warm in winter.
(e) A design to keep compact discs in order.
(f) A clean kitchen.

Generate a design

Think of ideas for a microwave meal. Develop and improve your ideas. Draw and model your designs. You might think about:
- what type of meal it will be
- what the package will look like
- what materials, ingredients and equipment will be used
- how to present the design
- how much it will cost
- how to improve the design
- how long it will take to make.

Record and present your results.

The design I chose for Snackspots

1. CARDBOARD CONTAINER, SPECIALLY SHAPED
2. EYECATCHING DESIGN/LOGO
3. COMPUTER BAR CODE
4. NUTRITIONAL INFORMATION AND INGREDIENTS
5. INSTRUCTIONS
6. PLASTIC CONTAINER RESISTS HIGH AND LOW TEMPERATURES

Planning and making

Plan and organise how you are going to make a microwave meal and then make it.

You might think about:
- how to make it
- what you will do first
- how you will use equipment
- how you will use materials and ingredients
- how to work quickly and safely.

Record and present your results.

What are needs and opportunities?

Is there a need?

There is a need:
- to satisfy hunger
- to find the way around a strange environment.

Is there an opportunity?

There might be a chance to:
- design something to eat
- design something to show directions.

Before you design and make something you might want to find out if there is a **need** for it. You could also find out if there is an **opportunity** to design and make it.

Activity

▶ What needs and opportunities would there be if someone said:
(a) 'I feel bored'
(b) 'I feel cold'
(c) 'I don't know what I've got to do tomorrow'?

What do we need?

People have many different needs:
- clothes for warmth
- air to breathe
- food to eat
- emotional needs such as love
- interests and hobbies
- to travel around
- tools and equipment for work and play
- a healthy environment
- a healthy diet
- to communicate with others.

Activity

▶ Make a list of all the things you need today.

▶ Compare your needs with those of someone else.
Are your needs similar or different?

Some of our needs - houses, a road system and a clean environment

Can we satisfy all our needs?

If you made a list of every one of your needs it would be very long.

You can't have everything you want. You have to **choose**.

Think of all the things you have bought in the last month. These could include magazines and clothes.

What is an opportunity?

People have many needs. There may be a **chance** to design and make something to satisfy these needs. If there is a chance we say that an opportunity exists.

People living in inner cities may want to live in a more healthy environment. There may be an opportunity to improve their surroundings.

There are many things you could do to improve this environment

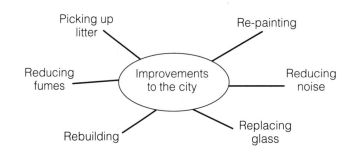

Picking up litter — Re-painting — Reducing fumes — Improvements to the city — Reducing noise — Rebuilding — Replacing glass

Are there always opportunities for design?

Whether there is an opportunity or not to design and make something depends on many things.
- Is it needed?
- Is it suitable?
- Does it cost too much?
- Does it already exist?
- Can it be changed?
- Is it possible to design and make it?
- Are there materials and equipment that can be used?

There might be an opportunity to make a 10 foot pen. It would not be needed for writing.
What could it be used for?

People might need a railway line from every town to every other town. Is there an opportunity to do this?

Activity

▶ Is there a need and an opportunity to design:
  (a) a railway line between all towns in the UK
  (b) a ten foot biro
  (c) a bus every minute on your local route
  (d) five postal deliveries a day to your house
  (e) paper clothing?

▶ What things do you think are needed in your classroom?
  Are there opportunities to design and make them?

The first computers were huge and expensive. This Moscow computer in 1955 could carry out 7,500 calculations a second. Why couldn't computers be used in the home in 1955?

Why do people have different needs?

Do you have the same needs as your parents or your friends? It is unlikely that you will eat the same food as a young baby or wear the same clothes as an old aged pensioner. Do you think that pregnant women and disabled people have the same needs?

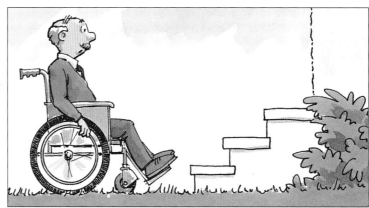

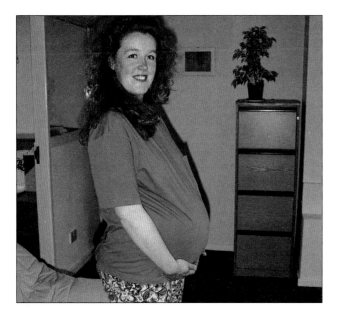

Activity

▶ Investigate the needs of the following under the headings eating, transport, exercise, recreation and clothing.
The drawing and the photograph may give you ideas.
(a) A baby.
(b) A teenager.
(c) A disabled adult.
(d) A pregnant woman.
Record and present your results.

▶ Discuss designs that could help them.
Draw or write your designs.

People from different cultures have different needs. A traditional Chinese meal will be different from a traditional English meal. Workers in hot climates often wear loose, white clothes.

A worker in Indonesia

Activity

▶ How have the needs of other cultures influenced your own?
The spider diagram and the photograph may give you some ideas.
Make a list under the headings:
(a) clothes
(b) food
(c) music.

▶ Present your results to the class.
You could use photographs, magazines and drawings to illustrate your ideas.

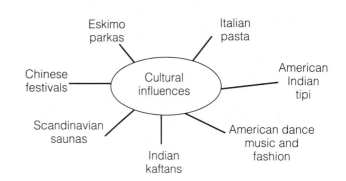

How needs change in different places

People's needs change depending on where they live. Needs will be different in different parts of a country. Your needs will change if you go to other countries, perhaps on holiday.

Activity

▶ Discuss your needs if you went on holiday to:
  (a) Spain in summer
  (b) Austria in winter
  (c) the seaside in autumn
  (d) climb mountains in spring.

▶ What designs might satisfy your needs?
Draw or write your ideas.

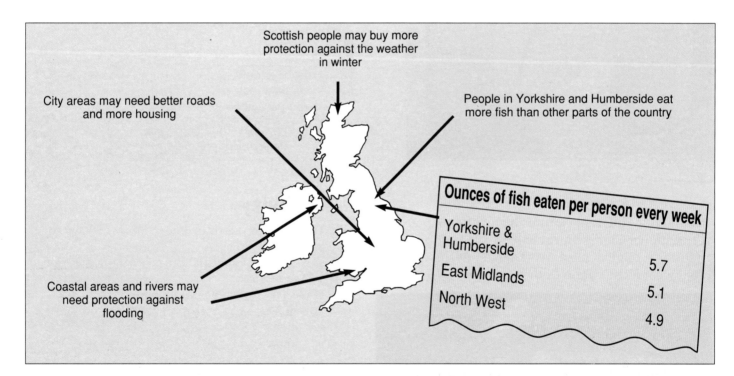

Scottish people may buy more protection against the weather in winter

City areas may need better roads and more housing

People in Yorkshire and Humberside eat more fish than other parts of the country

Coastal areas and rivers may need protection against flooding

Ounces of fish eaten per person every week	
Yorkshire & Humberside	5.7
East Midlands	5.1
North West	4.9

Activity

▶ Investigate what people need in different parts of the country
or
investigate what different areas need.
To do this you could:
- ask friends or relatives who live in other areas what they buy most
- look in geography books to get ideas of the things that certain areas need
- ask teachers who have lived in other areas
- write to local authority councils.

▶ Record and present your results.
You could use a map and photographs.
The diagram above might help you.

▶ Are the needs of different people or areas the same?
Discuss why they might be different.

▶ Draw a map of your local area.
Place shops, supermarkets, parks and factories on it.
Why do you think the shops, parks and businesses are found in these places?

How needs change over time

Needs and opportunities for design change over time. In medieval times people selling things would travel to the local market on animals and carts. Today goods are carried by aircraft to be sold abroad.

Notice how different the kitchens in the photographs look. One is from 1900. The other is from 1991.

Two kitchens built 91 years apart. Notice how they have changed in equipment, style, materials, safety, hygiene and use of energy.

Activity

▶ How have the following changed over the years:
  (a) kitchens
  (b) shopping
  (c) clothes
  (d) travel
  (e) how people communicate?

▶ What new needs have come from these changes?

▶ Even the time of day changes your needs. What do you need at:
  (a) 9am; (b) 11.30am; (c) 3.30pm; (d) 9pm; (e) 3am?

What we are doing

Our needs change depending on what we are doing. The boots designed for walking on the moon are very different from your trainers. Sunglasses are different from reading glasses.

You can change your designs so they can be used in different ways and new situations. Space technology is a good example of this.

Activity

▶ Write down all the design features of space travel shown in the picture.

▶ Investigate how each is now used on earth. Find information in books and magazines. Write away for information and ask others for their ideas.

▶ What needs do these designs meet?

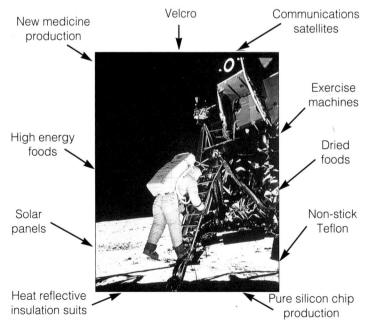

New medicine production

Velcro

Communications satellites

Exercise machines

Dried foods

Non-stick Teflon

Pure silicon chip production

Heat reflective insulation suits

Solar panels

High energy foods

Features of space travel

Designing something new

Sometimes you will have to design and make something new to satisfy people's needs. You can create designs that have not been made before.

Some new designs are called **inventions**. You can probably think of many examples in everyday life.

Activity

▶ What needs are satisfied by the designs on this page?

▶ Make a list of 10 inventions from the last 100 years.
Discuss the needs they have satisfied.

▶ Investigate the need for the following:
(a) a new way to get to school
(b) a new type of biscuit
(c) a new type of fuel.
You could interview your friends or neighbours.
Record and present your results.
You could use a questionnaire.
Try writing a questionnaire using a word processing program.

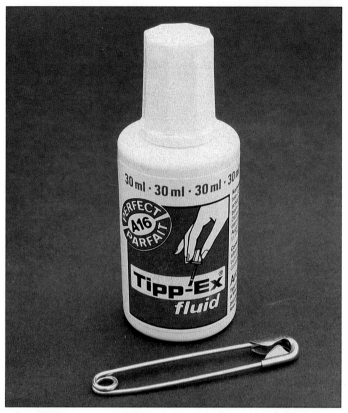

Liquid paper and the safety pin
Liquid paper is used to 'white out' mistakes. Before it was invented people had to rub out ink with a hard rubber.
The safety pin was invented by the Romans. Since then people have found it satisfies many needs.

High rise flats
A new environment created for people whose inner city houses were knocked down.

The fax machine
A new system of communication. Messages are sent on one fax and are printed out on another. Messages are carried between the two machines over a telephone line.

Adapting designs

You might be able to **improve** a design or **adapt** an old design.

People may already be using something but there may be a need to improve it. Meals are often changed to reduce the amount of fat in them. Road safety may be improved by adding a cycle track or a pelican crossing.

Sometimes 'old fashioned' designs which have been forgotten can be adapted and used again to satisfy today's needs. New clothes fashions can be old designs that have been changed into modern styles to suit today's needs.

Removable sticky notes started life as a glue that didn't stick! The design was changed so that notes could be removed without causing damage.

School meals have been adapted and improved. Rice, fruit and yoghurt are now offered as alternatives to chips and puddings.

The hypocaust system was used by Romans to heat houses and baths. Today's central heating system is similar to this.

The Forth cantilever bridge in Scotland (top) and the Clifton suspension bridge at Bristol. Bridge designs were changed to meet different needs.

Activity

► What needs are satisfied by the designs on this page?

► Investigate the need for:
  (a) a girl's school uniform with trousers
  (b) white writing pens on a blackboard
  (c) different coloured food.
  Record and present your results.

► Investigate the need to improve:
  (a) the queuing system at the Post Office
  (b) school meals
  (c) television programmes between 5-6 o'clock
  (d) local street lighting.
  Record and present your results.

► Drinks machines are found in places like train stations.
  Investigate where else they might be needed in your local area.
  Record and present your results.

► Look through history books.
  What designs could be used today?
  What needs would be satisfied?

Identifying the problem

You design and make things to solve problems. Solving the problems will satisfy people's needs. You must find out what the problem is first. Then you can decide what to design and make.

PROBLEM PAGE

My little sister is too big for her high chair but too small to sit at the table in one of the normal chairs.

I need a packed lunch for a museum visit but my bag is not very big.

I'm having a party in the garden. It starts at two o'clock but we don't want to eat until three.

My doctor has told me to avoid using butter and margarine but I don't like dry bread.

When I sunbathe I always end up sliding down the lounger because it's too slippery!

When I'm sitting at my computer I have to walk across the room to my filing cabinet for disks.

Grandad is very old. He finds it difficult to sit comfortably and sit up straight at a table. He can't eat tough or fatty foods.

How will you solve these problems?

You have made the meal and chair below to help him.

TOAST CHIPS WARM SOUP WARM DRINK SPAGHETTI DOUGHNUTS

GOLD PLATED WOOD

Constraints

There are **limits** or **constraints** on the things you design. If you were designing the meal for grandad on the opposite page you would choose food that is **suitable** for an old person's needs.

There are many other constraints on your designs.

Time – How long do you have to design and make it?

Cost – Will it cost too much?

Size and shape – Will it fit? What size does it have to be?

Resources – What materials, ingredients, tools and equipment are needed? Are they available?

Fashion – Does it have to be a certain style?

Colour – Does it have to be a certain colour?

Skills – Can you make it on your own? Should you work with people who have other skills?

Health and safety – Will it be safe to use? Will it be healthy?

Convenience foods

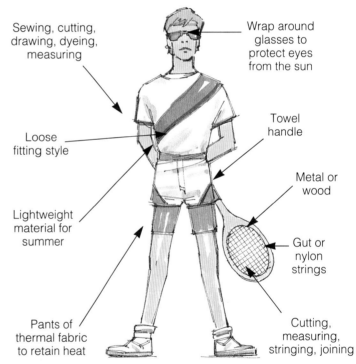

Sewing, cutting, drawing, dyeing, measuring

Wrap around glasses to protect eyes from the sun

Loose fitting style

Towel handle

Metal or wood

Lightweight material for summer

Gut or nylon strings

Pants of thermal fabric to retain heat

Cutting, measuring, stringing, joining

Windmill herb rack

1 dressed pine 120 x 45 x 120 mm (5 x 2 nom x 4⅞ in)
1 dressed pine 45 x 20 x 75 mm (2 x 1 nom x 3 in)
1 screw and nut set with countersunk head 6 mm diameter, 75 mm long (¼ in diameter, 3 in long)
8 round-headed screws (No. 8) 20 mm (¾ in)
2 countersunk screws (for wall-mounting) (No. 8) 45 mm (2 in)
8 glass jars with screw-top lids
'Twin-pack' adhesive
PVA woodworker's adhesive
Varnish

Activity

▶ Make a list of the constraints on the designs on this page.
Present it to the class for discussion.

▶ Discuss the constraints on the following designs.
(a) A ruler to fit into your pencil case.
(b) A meal for a vegetarian or vegan.
(c) An electronic alarm for your school bag.
(d) A place for an animal to stay in the house.
(e) A database to keep the names and addresses of local businesses.
(f) A shopping centre.
Record your ideas.

Writing a design brief

A design brief is a **short** sentence or a few sentences saying what you are going to do.

The design brief includes:
- the needs you are satisfying
- what you are designing and making
- any constraints.

My mother thinks that our family eats too much fatty food. She wants us to eat fewer chips and dairy products. She also wants to stop frying food in fat. We are cooking a meal today, but my mother does not want to spend more than £6 on the ingredients.

Design brief

Design and make a low fat meal for a family that does not cost more than £6.

I have asked people in the doctor's surgery about seating in the waiting room. Young people think it is alright but old people are not very happy. They say that the chairs are too hard and they get sore after sitting for more than five minutes. Doctor Phillips has asked me to think of ideas to make the chairs more comfortable.

Design brief

Design and make a chair that an old person can sit on comfortably.

Activity

▶ Write a design brief for each of the students' notes below.

I am going to a party. I only have £3 pocket money and I need a new bracelet to wear.

As a class we have researched the hall, looking at fire safety. Our group studied the stage. Underneath there were loads of boxes full of flammable props. We want to design and make a fireproof box to put them in.

School uniforms are old - fashioned and boring. I want to design a new trendy uniform that both students and teachers will like. We will only have time to go as far as the mock up stage.

My friends told me they needed to make breakfast quickly on Saturday morning. Most thought it should contain fibre and, if possible, fruit.

People who are deaf cannot hear a door bell ring. I want to make a doorbell for a deaf person using my knowledge of electronics. Mrs Smith has said that we have until Easter to complete the work and it is now November.

Traffic is very heavy on one road into our town centre. I want to design a model to show how a different route would ease town congestion. I found out that there is a council meeting in 5 weeks where I can explain my ideas.

Design specifications and analysis

After you have written a design brief there are still many choices for you to make.

You must pick out the main parts of the design brief. These are the **design specifications**.

Looking closely at each specification is called **analysis**. For each specification you must decide what things to think about and what to do.

Here are the specifications and analysis for the chair and the meal on the opposite page. You will see that some of the analysis is missing.

Specifications	Analysis of a low fat family meal
Design	
Make	
Low fat	
Meal	
Family	
Cost	Where can I buy food cheapest? What is the cheapest food I can buy?

Specifications and analysis of a family meal. The analysis shows questions that you might ask.

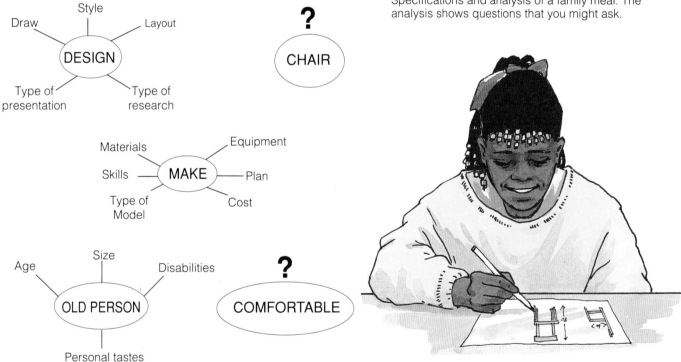

Specifications and analysis of a comfortable chair. The analysis shows things that you might think about.

Developing and improving your design

Ideas for your design can be developed in many ways. You can:
- generate your own ideas
- ask other people for their ideas
- sketch and draw different designs
- make a model and test it
- role play.

You have been asked to design something safe or warm for a child aged between one and three. When writing or drawing your design you might think about some of the following things.

Here are some of the ideas you might have generated for your design.

Activity

▶ Design something safe or warm for a child. You will have to:
- generate and record different ideas for design
- ask others for their views on your ideas and record their comments
- write or draw many different design ideas.
You could model your design in suitable materials, on computer, with a modelling kit or modelling materials.

▶ Design one or more of the following:
(a) a 'space' costume for a play
(b) a Chinese kite
(c) a ramp for a wheelchair in your school
(d) a sports kit
(e) a local sports arena
(f) a test to see how quick your reactions are or how strong you are
(g) a way to show someone how to swim
(h) a drink for someone who is allergic to caffeine
or any of your designs on page 20.

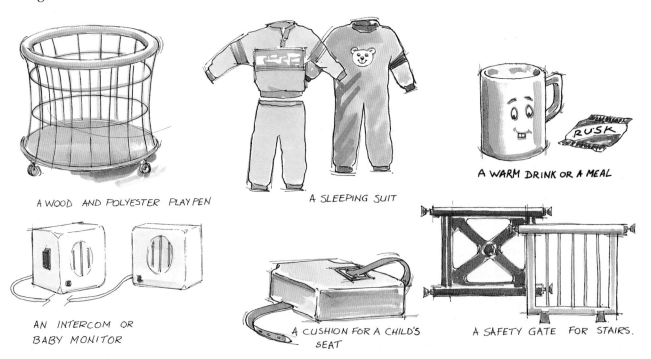

A WOOD AND POLYESTER PLAY PEN

A SLEEPING SUIT

A WARM DRINK OR A MEAL

AN INTERCOM OR BABY MONITOR

A CUSHION FOR A CHILD'S SEAT

A SAFETY GATE FOR STAIRS.

You will have to choose which design to use. You might pick the wood and polyester play pen.

You then need to:
- improve your ideas - **refining**
- give reasons for your choices - **justifying.**

Your play pen might look like the design below. You can see that the ideas have been refined and justified.

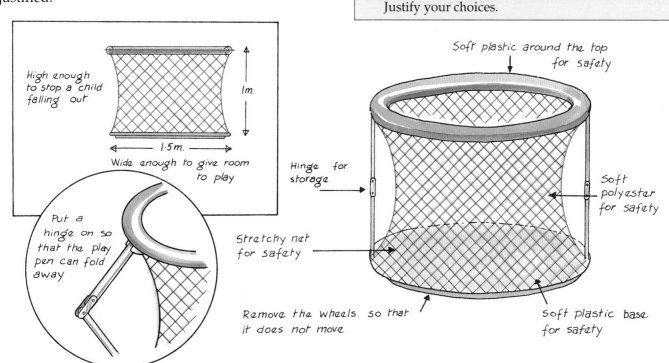

High enough to stop a child falling out

1m.

1·5m.

Wide enough to give room to play

Put a hinge on so that the play pen can fold away

Soft plastic around the top for safety

Hinge for storage

Stretchy net for safety

Soft polyester for safety

Remove the wheels so that it does not move

Soft plastic base for safety

You have been asked to design a school bag with an animal theme. Here are some ideas. One design has been chosen and refined.

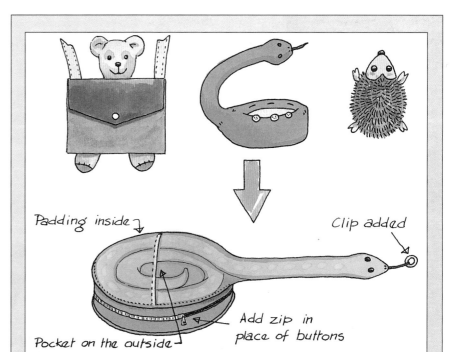

Padding inside

Clip added

Pocket on the outside

Add zip in place of buttons

Refining a bag with an animal theme

A design proposal

A design proposal is the final stage before you make your design. It is a very accurate drawing or number of drawings showing all the features of the design. It shows exactly what you are going to do.

Sometimes you need to change or **edit** your design proposal. The spider diagram gives some reasons why.

Design does not satisfy a need

Cost is too great

Materials are not suitable

Why you edit your design

Not enough resources

Design is too complicated

Design does not work

Activity

▶ What things are being designed on this page?

▶ Evaluate the design proposals.
  Will they work?
  Think about cost, size, type of materials and shape.

▶ Change one of the designs.
  Draw or model your new design.

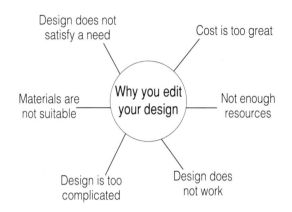

Leonardo Da Vinci's proposal for flight in 1486

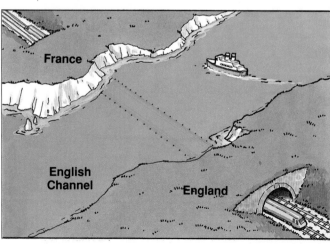

In 1988 it was thought the Channel Tunnel would cost £5 billion. By 1990 this was £8 billion.

Generating a design

This chapter has shown you how to generate a design. Imagine that you have been given a job as part of a design team. Below is the work that has come in this week.

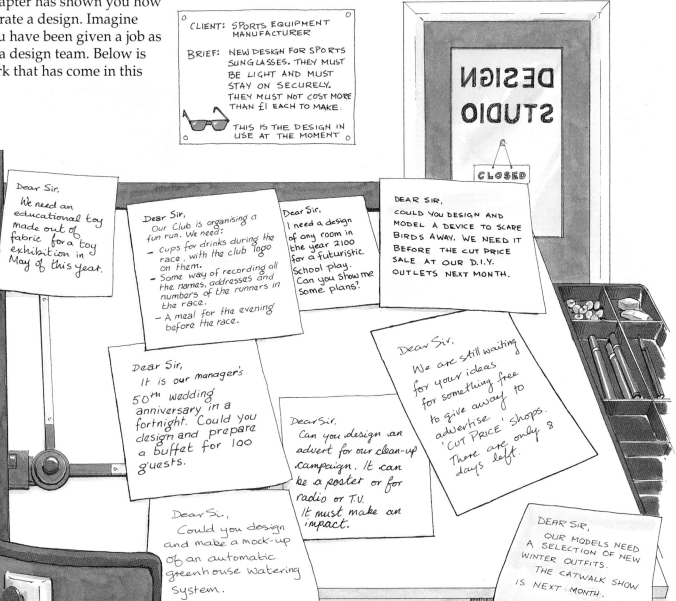

CLIENT: SPORTS EQUIPMENT MANUFACTURER

BRIEF: NEW DESIGN FOR SPORTS SUNGLASSES. THEY MUST BE LIGHT AND MUST STAY ON SECURELY. THEY MUST NOT COST MORE THAN £1 EACH TO MAKE.

THIS IS THE DESIGN IN USE AT THE MOMENT

Dear Sir,
We need an educational toy made out of fabric for a toy exhibition in May of this year.

Dear Sir,
Our Club is organising a fun run. We need:
- cups for drinks during the race, with the club logo on them.
- Some way of recording all the names, addresses and numbers of the runners in the race.
- A meal for the evening before the race.

Dear Sir,
I need a design of any room in the year 2100 for a futuristic school play. Can you show me some plans?

DEAR SIR,
COULD YOU DESIGN AND MODEL A DEVICE TO SCARE BIRDS AWAY. WE NEED IT BEFORE THE CUT PRICE SALE AT OUR D.I.Y. OUTLETS NEXT MONTH.

Dear Sir,
It is our manager's 50th wedding anniversary in a fortnight. Could you design and prepare a buffet for 100 guests.

Dear Sir,
Can you design an advert for our clean-up campaign. It can be a poster or for radio or T.V. It must make an impact.

Dear Sir,
We are still waiting for your ideas for something free to give away to advertise 'CUT PRICE' shops. There are only 8 days left.

Dear Sir,
Could you design and make a mock-up of an automatic greenhouse watering system.

DEAR SIR,
OUR MODELS NEED A SELECTION OF NEW WINTER OUTFITS. THE CATWALK SHOW IS NEXT MONTH.

DESIGN STUDIO

CLOSED

Activity

- ▶ Choose one of the problems above.
- ▶ Pick out the constraints.
  Who is the design for?
  Do you know the cost?
  What materials you will need?
  What other constraints are there?
- ▶ Write a design brief.

- ▶ Write out the design specifications and analysis.
- ▶ Develop your design by generating ideas, drawing, modelling and asking for opinions.
- ▶ Choose the best design.
- ▶ Refine and justify your choices.
- ▶ Present a design proposal.
  Edit it if you have to.

Planning

Have you ever planned and organised a trip to the swimming baths or the park with your friends?

What would you do if you were planning a visit this week? You would have to decide how long things will take. You might spend five minutes packing your bag. You would decide which things were most important and which to do first.

This is called **prioritising**. You might call for a friend living next door before anyone else.

If the baths are closed when you arrive the plan would not have been **effective**. Well organised plans satisfy our needs. You need to get to the baths on time. A well organised plan or **production schedule** will help you to do this.

Start getting ready at 9.00 a.m. on Saturday. Take five minutes to pack your bags.

Call for your friends.

Wait for the bus.
Travel on the bus.

Arrive at the swimming baths.

Activity

► Plan a visit with a friend.
  - Write out the tasks in order.
  - Decide how long each task should take.
  - Present your plan as a time plan, flow chart, storyboard or on a computer.
  - Try it out.
  - Does the plan work?
  - If it does not work, how could you improve it?

► Design and present a plan for:
  - making a salad
  - making a mask for a festival.

The plans have been started for you across the page.
Finish them off.

Take out the food (4 mins)
↓
Hard boil the eggs (6 mins)
↓
Wash the lettuce (3 mins)

Draw around my head (5 mins)
↓
Design the mask (1 hour)
↓
Cut out the template (10 mins)

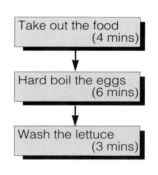

Planning and making a salad

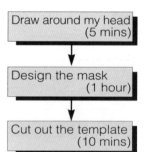

Planning and making a mask

Choosing materials and equipment

When you plan to make something you have to choose which tools, equipment and materials to use.

You must choose tools and equipment that will help you to make things:

- easily
- accurately
- safely
- quickly.

┌─ **Activity** ─────────────────────────┐

▶ What tools and equipment would you need to:
(a) join together pieces of cloth
(b) strip plastic covering from insulating wire
(c) make a model of your bedroom in wood or card
(d) cook rice
(e) make a new filing system
(f) show the layout of a buffet
(g) make a logo for a tee shirt
(h) make a night light?
The drawings below will give you some ideas.

When choosing materials you will need to think about their **properties** - the things they can or can not do. You can twist and bend rubber, cotton fabric or dough, but only rubber will bounce.

┌─ **Activity** ─────────────────────────┐

▶ Discuss and record the materials you would and would not choose to:
(a) make a magazine
(b) build a floating model
(c) make a fireproof box
(d) prevent draughts in your house
(e) make a meal for an active teenager.

▶ Discuss and record the properties of the materials you chose in the question above.
Now do the same for those you did not choose.

▶ What materials and equipment would you choose to make an athletics kit and skateboard equipment?
The pictures opposite will give you some ideas.

What skills do you need?

You need skills to make things. If you don't have the skills you will have to learn them. Sometimes it is easier to work with someone who has them. The skills we have affect the materials and equipment we choose.

Activity

▶ Record the skills you think you have.
Ask your friends to comment on your list.

▶ Discuss the skills that the people in these pictures have. What artefacts, systems and environments could they make?

▶ What skills would you need to make the designs on p. 27?

Workers on a building site

A doctor testing a patient's health

Sewing fabric

A computer operator

Cooking food

Welding metal

Safety

There are always dangers when making things. You need to plan how you will make things very carefully. This will help you to avoid accidents.

Activity

▶ Identify the dangers in the pictures above.

▶ Discuss how they could affect the materials and equipment that were chosen.

▶ Plan how to avoid the dangers.

Cost and availability

When choosing how to plan and make your designs you must ask yourself:
- can I get hold of materials and equipment
- where can I buy them cheapest
- what are the cheapest?

Buying the cheapest things will save money, but the cheapest things may not always be the best for your design.

Activity

▶ You have designed an electronic clock that will run on one R6 battery.
Look at the battery prices.
Where would you buy the cheapest battery and how much would you pay?

▶ Which battery will last the longest?

▶ Which batteries give the best value for money?
Where would you buy them and how much would you pay?

▶ Make a list of designs that would use:
(a) zinc chloride batteries
(b) alkaline batteries.

	Zinc chloride — Best for products which do not need a lot of electricity.		Alkaline — Best for products which are used a lot or use a lot of power. Tests have shown they last more than twice as long as other batteries.	
Boots	1.39		2.59	
Car accessory shop	1.60	1.39	2.96	2.60
Chemist (independent)	1.45	1.35	3.07	2.50
Corner store	1.80	1.53	3.50	2.60
Currys	not sold		2.79	
Department store	1.45	1.30	2.95	2.25
Dixons	not sold		2.79	
Electrical shop	1.44	1.28	2.92	2.40
Hardware store	1.60	1.39	3.04	2.69
Newsagent	1.42	1.37	2.69	2.66
Photographic store	1.45	1.44	2.76	2.69
Rumbelows	1.42		2.59	
Supermarket	1.40	1.35	2.59	2.49

Source: adapted from *Which?* magazine.

The highest and lowest R6 battery prices

Aesthetics

Your designs must look right. The materials and colours you choose will affect how your design looks. You may choose a colour because it looks nice or because it is useful. Bright colours show up at night. This helps to avoid accidents.

Activity

▶ Why do you think the colours in the photographs opposite were chosen?

▶ Plan to make:
(a) a mobile for a young child
(b) a topping for a carrot cake
(c) a disco light show
(d) a shirt or top for a night out.
Draw your designs.
What colours would you choose?

Knights at a medieval theme park

A computer screen

Measuring up

Before making something you need to know if there is enough material or if there are enough ingredients. If you are using too much then you are **wasting** material.

To avoid waste, measure out how much is needed. Sometimes you will **mark out** on the material. Sometimes you will measure or weigh ingredients. Some examples of measuring designs are shown across the page.

Activity

▶ Look at the carpet measurements across the page. How much carpet would you need to:
  (a) make a doormat
  (b) cover your classroom
  (c) cover the stairs in your house?
  How much waste would you have?

▶ How many of the sweet packet designs across the page can you mark out onto an A4 sheet of paper? How much waste do you have? How could you avoid waste?

▶ Plan how to make the recipe for Chinese fried rice. How would you measure the ingredients? How could you avoid waste?

▶ If you were making a book you would measure different widths and sizes of letters, photographs, spaces and the size of pages. Measure different things on this page. Are other pages the same?

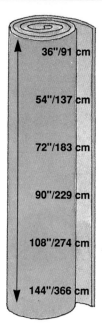

Rolls of carpet are sold at different widths. They can be cut to any length. In Britain widths are usually shown in inches.

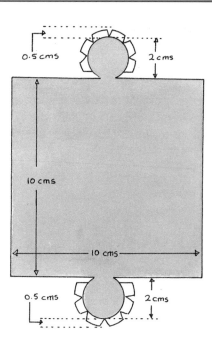

Sweet packets can be made using different designs

CHINESE FRIED RICE

3 tablespoons of oil	125g peeled prawns
4 Chopped onions	50g cooked ham
125g mushrooms	50g frozen peas
3 eggs beaten	1-2 tablespoons of
250g cooked rice	soy sauce

Recipes tell you the quantity and weight of the ingredients

You are planning to design a gymnasium like the one in the photograph.

Activity

▶ What things will you measure?

▶ Draw a plan of the gym and write in the measurements.

▶ What measures would you take if you were going to:
  (a) change your route to school
  (b) change someone's diet
  (c) change a hairstyle?

Cutting

When you have your hair cut the hairdresser will use scissors, electric trimmers and perhaps even a razor. When you make something you cut materials with special tools and equipment. It is important that you choose the right tools. You often cut materials to **shape** or **size**.

You can cut:
- fabrics such as cotton or denim
- materials such as elastic, wood, metal and plastic
- food ingredients such as spaghetti, cheese or apples.

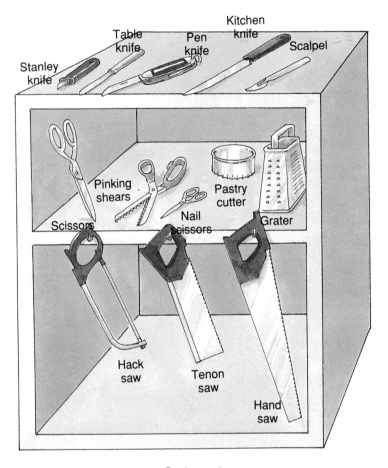

Cutting tools

Activity

▶ What tools in the drawing would you use to:
- cut card
- cut wood
- shape pastry
- make coleslaw
- shape cotton fabric?

▶ Try cutting the materials above.
What problems did you have?
Did you choose the best tools?

▶ Design a test to see how straight you can cut.
Evaluate your test.

▶ How can you cut the same shape out many times?
Design a test and evaluate it.

Industries and businesses use many different methods to cut materials. The photographs across the page show how crops and metal are cut.

Activity

▶ Choose an industry or a business.
You might choose the building, agricultural or motor car industry.
You could choose a bakery or a manufacturer of clothing or magazines.

▶ Discuss the materials that are used when making things.

▶ Investigate how materials are cut.
You could write for information or look in textbooks and magazines.

▶ What problems do they find?
How do they solve them?

Folding and bending

You can also make shapes by folding and bending. Folding materials in different ways will change your designs.

Activity

▶ What types of materials are being folded in the pictures?

▶ What tools would you use to fold these materials?

▶ Select tools to help you.
Try folding or bending some of the materials.
How can you change the things you make?

▶ What problems did you have? How could you solve them?

Assembling

Before you join materials together you have to place them in the right position. They have to be held in that position until they can be fixed. This is called assembling.

Activity

▶ What tools and equipment would you choose to assemble:
(a) a mock-up of a coat
(b) a wooden frame?
The photographs and the drawing may give you some ideas.

▶ Try holding together different materials. You could try holding plastic, muslin or icing on a cake.
What problems did you have?
How could you solve them?

▶ Assemble the following so they do not move:
(a) a corner frame using card or straws
(b) photographs onto a design of a book cover, on card or on a computer.
What problems would you have if they had moved?

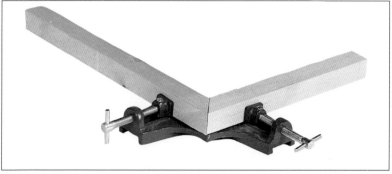

Joining

Materials can be joined together in many ways. You need to decide which way is suitable for your designs. Some joints cannot be moved. These are **permanent** joints. Other joints allow movement.

Ways to join materials together

Activity

▶ Discuss how the things in the picture across the page join materials together.

▶ Which are permanent and which allow movement?

▶ Think of ten ways to join two pieces of card or paper.
Which are permanent and which allow movement?

▶ Try joining together:
- card to allow movement
- wood permanently
- wire permanently.
What did you use?
How successful were you?

Mixing

Materials can also be joined together by mixing. You can mix two or more ingredients or materials together when making your designs. Try experimenting with different amounts. Different types of bread can be made by changing the ingredients. You could make garlic bread or wholemeal bread. Colours can be changed by adding different amounts of paint.

Activity

▶ Look at the materials being mixed below.
What equipment would you use to mix them?
How could mixing these materials help when making a design?

▶ Choose materials or ingredients to mix together. You could try mixing together the materials in the drawings or choose some of your own.
- Check with your teacher for safety.
- Choose the equipment you will use.
- Mix the materials.
- Experiment with different quantities and different materials.
- Design a test to evaluate how well the materials mix.
- Record all your results.

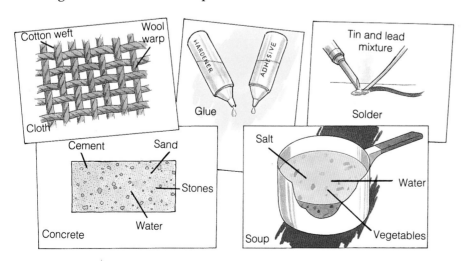

Finishing

Once you have made something there are still rough edges and loose materials to tidy up or smooth off. We call this finishing.

We can also finish by painting or glazing our designs. Finishing makes a design look more attractive. Why is this important?

Activity

▶ How are materials being finished in the photographs opposite?

▶ Try different paints on card.
Which gives the best finish?

▶ Try the same test on metal or other materials.
Which gives the best finish?

▶ Try different ways to:
- finish a birthday cake
- finish a plant pot made of terracotta.

Improvising

Even the best plans can go wrong. There are always problems when you make things. You don't have to give up! You can get around the problem with a little thought. You might be able to use other equipment and materials. You might be able to adapt what you are doing to suit new needs and opportunities. This is called improvising.

Activity

▶ Discuss how you would solve the problems below.

▶ Choose one problem.
Plan a solution.

▶ Present your solution to others and ask them to evaluate it.

I NEED TO DRILL A HOLE BUT I DON'T KNOW HOW TO OPERATE AN ELECTRIC DRILL.

THE BREAD I MADE HAS NOT RISEN.

I'VE BEEN ILL FOR THREE WEEKS. MY DESIGN HAS TO BE READY BY NEXT WEEK. WHAT SHOULD I DO?

I NEED TO SEND OUT 100 QUESTIONNAIRES BY TOMORROW.

I'VE ONLY GOT 50p LEFT. I STILL HAVE TO DECORATE MY CAKE.

WE ARE WRITING AND PERFORMING A SHORT PLAY. I NEED TO MAKE SURE EVERYONE IS DOING THE THINGS THEY ARE BEST AT.

NO MATTER WHAT I DO, THESE PIECES OF WOOD WON'T STICK TOGETHER WITH GLUE.

I'VE SENT OUT A QUESTIONNAIRE. I'VE RECORDED PEOPLE'S NAMES ON A DATABASE. NOW I NEED TO KNOW HOW MANY ARE CLOSE ENOUGH TO INTERVIEW.

Planning and making a design

You are part of a team working on a new magazine for teenagers or a school magazine. You will need to design your front cover and a page before you plan and make it. The pages below may give you some ideas.

Design your cover and page. You could use a word processing or desk top publishing program.
Next you must plan and make your design.

You will need to do these things.
- Decide on the order of tasks and approximate times for each one.
- Decide who is to do what and what skills are needed.
- Choose materials, tools and equipment that you need and find out their cost.
- Record your costs.
  You could use a spreadsheet.
- Measure the page and decide how many words you can fit on the page.
- Decide which colours to use.
- Decide on the size of the magazine and the number of pages it will have.
- Decide how many copies to make.
- Choose how to join the pages together.
- Find out the total cost to make the magazine.
- Decide how much to sell it for.
- Make the magazine.
- How did you solve any problems you found?

Activity

▶ Design, plan and make a magazine in a group. Make sure you carry out all the tasks on this page.
Record all your results.

▶ Choose one of the following.
Plan and make it in a group.
  (a) A wooden musical instrument.
  (b) A self-propelled child's toy boat.
  (c) A bottle bank for a cleaner environment in the park.
  (d) A four course evening meal for a family that doesn't eat meat.
  (e) A colour coded filing system for cassettes or CDs.
  (f) A costume for:
     - a Chinese festival
     - a Brazilian carnival
     - a Japanese or Indian play.
  (g) A window garden for an old aged pensioner.
  (h) A model with moving parts to show how a lock on a canal would work.

What is evaluation?

Think about the last time you:
- read a book or magazine
- saw a film, video or TV programme
- painted something
- drew a picture
- played a game or sport.

Afterwards you probably thought about what you liked and disliked.

You were **evaluating**.

When you design and make an artefact, system or environment you will evaluate its success. You will need to decide and judge how good it is and whether your ideas have worked.

A motor show

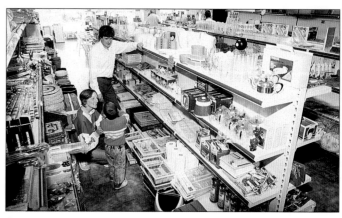
Shopping

Activity

▶ What things do you think the people in these pictures might be evaluating?

▶ Look at the ideas for things you might evaluate at the top of the page.
Choose one idea and write down what you liked and disliked about it.
You might choose to evaluate a video, a book or a game.

Tasting drinks

An archaeological dig

Comparing

Have you ever 'shopped around' for things? You might have looked for the 'best' trainers, the cheapest cut of meat or the brightest shirt or leggings. You could have compared different trainers before you chose to buy a pair.

Comparing means looking at the things which are similar and different about designs.

Activity

Compare the radios and radio cassettes below.

▶ What things are different about them?

▶ Which do you think is best?

▶ Which do you think would cost:
(a) the most
(b) the least?
Give reasons for your choices.

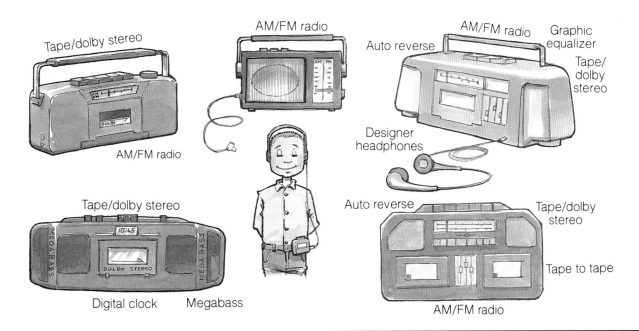

Tape/dolby stereo
AM/FM radio
AM/FM radio
Auto reverse
AM/FM radio
Graphic equalizer
Tape/dolby stereo
Designer headphones
Tape/dolby stereo
Digital clock
Megabass
Auto reverse
Tape/dolby stereo
Tape to tape
AM/FM radio

If you want to compare things in detail you could carry out a **survey**. You might look for information in shops or catalogues.

Activity

Visit a local shop or look in catalogues.

▶ Choose one product to evaluate.

▶ Compare the different brands or makes on sale.

▶ Record and present your results.
The 'Trainer Survey' might help you.
You could use a database or a spreadsheet.

▶ Which brand do you think is best?

▶ Why do you think it is best?

▶ Compare your results with another person's results.

TRAINER SURVEY

Make	Price	Features	Fashion	Comfort
Reebok				
Nike				
Adidas				
Ellesse				

Looking at the past and other cultures

You can also compare designs with things from the past.

Ice houses were used in nineteenth century housing. They were found outside the house and were used to keep things frozen for up to two years.

Modern refrigerators are designed to be used in the house. Food is usually stored for a shorter period of time.

Activity

▶ Compare the ice house and the refrigerator. You might think about the following things for each.
  - Is it cheap to make?
  - Is it cheap to run?
  - Would it fit in your kitchen?
  - How much will it hold?
  - Can the parts be recycled?
  - Is it hygienic and safe?
  - Is it easy to use?

Older models have CFC cooling systems

Freezer keeps food for up to 3 months

Compact

Storage space

Easy access

A modern refrigerator

Straw lined walls

Stone lining

Entrance

Large blocks of ice

An ice house

Pulley system

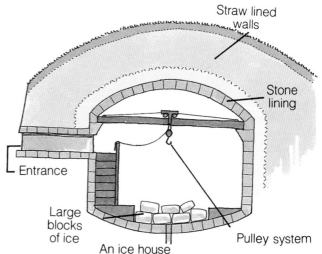

You can also compare designs with those of other cultures.

The sari is made from one piece of cloth. The cloth is folded around the body to make one piece of clothing. The same idea is used in other cultures. The Scottish plaid only uses one piece of material.

The design of an American Indian tipi was used in the design of modern tents. The design was improved and waterproof materials were used.

Activity

▶ Compare the sari to Western clothes.
  - Is it easy to make?
  - Does it keep you warm or cool?
  - Can you move easily?

▶ Compare the use of a tent on holiday to:
  (a) a caravan
  (b) a flat.

A sari and a Scottish plaid

Tent designs – an American Indian tipi and a modern tent

Opinions

You can evaluate by saying what you think about a design.

You will have your own **opinions** and make your own **judgements** about the artefacts, systems and environments that have been made. You can also ask others for their opinions.

When you evaluate your designs you will take into account many things. We call these things **criteria**. Imagine that you have designed a new washing powder called Washo. How would you evaluate its success? Some of the things you might think about are shown across the page.

SAFETY. IS IT HARMFUL TO THE USER OR THE ENVIRONMENT?

DOES IT SATISFY A NEED?

DOES IT MEET THE DESIGN BRIEF?

COST/PRICE. IS IT CHEAP TO MAKE?

DOES IT WORK WELL? DOES IT WASH CLEAN?

DOES IT LOOK NICE?

DOES IT SMELL NICE? DOES IT FEEL NICE?

Evaluating a washing powder

A fruit salad

A recycled plastic bag

An 'early' design for a flying machine

A cheap holiday to London

A modern kettle

Activity

▶ You have designed and made the five items in the drawings across the page.
  - Evaluate the designs.
  - Write down all the things you would take into account when evaluating them.
  - Do you think the designs are successful?

▶ Look at the photograph of cycle equipment below.
  - Evaluate the equipment.
  - What things would you take into account?
  - Design your own cycle equipment.
  - Ask others to evaluate it and record their comments.

Cycle equipment

Testing and trying out

You can evaluate your design by testing it and trying it out. This might mean doing an **experiment** or asking someone to use it.

You will be able to find out:
- if it works
- how well it works
- if it satisfies the need you identified
- if it meets the design brief
- if it is safe.

A climbing frame

Activity

▶ How would you test whether the designs in these three photographs were successful?

▶ Design and make a puzzle, such as a tangram, a crossword or any other puzzle.
You could use a computer or an electronic system.
- Test it on a friend.
- Record the results of the test.
- Evaluate its success.

A computer program or game

Trying on new clothes

Your test or trial will tell you things about your design. It may not satisfy the need you identified. It may not work as you would have liked.

You will need to change parts of the design. We call this **modifying**. Across the page are a number of designs. They do not satisfy the needs you identified. These needs are shown underneath each design.

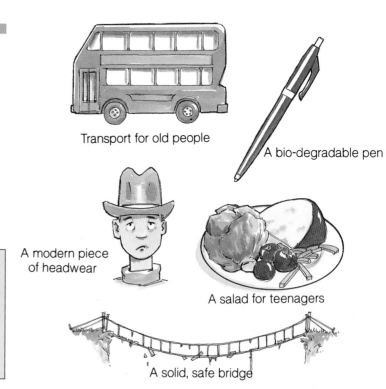

Transport for old people

A bio-degradable pen

A modern piece of headwear

A salad for teenagers

A solid, safe bridge

Activity

▶ Choose one design.

▶ Modify your design to meet the need shown below it.

▶ Draw or write your new designs.

▶ How would you test your new designs?

Putting yourself in someone else's shoes

You can evaluate your designs by looking at a problem from someone else's **point of view**. You may find your evaluation will be very different.

Imagine you are deaf. A bell for a fire alarm would not be a very successful design from your point of view.

A small car may be easy to drive and park, but a tall person may find it cramped inside and difficult to get into.

Activity

▶ Evaluate the designs across the page from the point of view of:
(a)   a person who is blind
(b)   an old aged pensioner
(c)   someone in a wheelchair
(d)   a Muslim family who speak little English and don't eat pork.
Present your results.

▶ How would you modify the designs to overcome the problems?
Draw, write or model your designs.

▶ Carry out a role play exercise to evaluate how a blind person might cope in your school.
What designs could help them?

Today many green field sites are being built on. People need houses but they also want countryside.

Houses being built on countryside

Activity

A firm is building new houses on land in your area. Carry out a role play exercise. Act out what might happen. Here are the rules.

▶ Break up into two groups.
One group should act as the firm.
The other should act as local people.

▶ Evaluate the arguments for and against the building of houses.

▶ Prepare a five minute talk for and against the plans.

▶ Act out a meeting of the two groups.

▶ Vote on whether the building should take place.

▶ Record and present your results.

Reviewing

You can look back at **each stage** of the design and production process and evaluate it. This is called reviewing.

Research - did it tell you what you wanted to know?

Design - did it suit the purpose?

Plan - how well did it work?
- what problems did it have?

Making - did you choose suitable tools and materials?
- did you work safely?
- did you use the best method?
- did you have the skills?

Activity

Look at the two case studies below.
Imagine you are the technology student.

▶ Evaluate what you did.
What problems were there?

▶ Suggest changes that you would make next time.

▶ Ask others for their views.
You could use a questionnaire or an interview.

Case study - organising a festival

I am helping to organise a festival to show the things our local area produces. We have hired a hall and laid on an 'English type' buffet for 100 people. The local Chinese community has offered to decorate the hall. We have advertised in the local paper for a day. We asked our friends what we should show at the exhibition and they said to concentrate on things for young people.

Case study - building a model

I have built a model to show how water can be diverted in developing countries to irrigate land. My model uses a system of gates, levers and pulleys. I have used a plastic base, with card and string for the gates and pulleys. The plastic base has two grooves which are used as rivers. The sides are not steep enough. Water spills out before it reaches the gates.

One of the problems you will face is that the needs you identified at the start may **change** as you make your design. You will have to evaluate the **final design** to see if it still meets a need.

Roads are a good example of this. As more people bought cars there was a need for more roads. This reduced the safety of pedestrians. Roads then had to be redesigned to meet these different needs. Some roads had pedestrian walkways built over them. You can see this in the photographs.

Activity

▶ How have the needs of road users changed?

▶ How might roads be changed to meet people's needs?

▶ How can road traffic be reduced?
Present your own ideas.
Ask others for their ideas.

How did I do?

Redesigning a classroom

After you have played a game you often think about your own feelings. How did I do? This is **personal evaluation**. If you are part of a group redesigning your classroom you may ask the questions above.

It is important when designing and making to record your attitudes and feelings about yourself. You will be able to pick out any problems you had. You will also be able to decide how to be more successful next time. You can record what you feel on a **personal profile**.

Activity

▶ Write a profile to evaluate:
  (a) your handwriting
  (b) how well you remember things
  (c) how tidy your room is.

▶ Write out your own personal profile.
  You could complete one of the two shown across the page.

▶ What other ways can you think of to present your profile?
  Think about using a colour code or a computer.

▶ Use the profile you have written to record your attitudes when designing, planning and making:
  - a tidy kitchen
  - a speech on road safety at assembly
  - a low fat snack
  - a card, plastic or wood model of a building.

PERSONAL PROFILE 1

I remembered all my equipment ☺ 😐 ☹

I was able to start work with little or no instruction ☺ 😐 ☹

I was able to follow and carry out instructions ☺ 😐 ☹

My work was neat, tidy and attractively presented ☺ 😐 ☹

PERSONAL PROFILE 2

TASK	VERY EASY	EASY	OK	HARD	VERY HARD	COMMENTS
ORGANISING MY WORK						
FOLLOWING INSTRUCTIONS						
MOTIVATION AND INTEREST						

Two ways of recording your personal profile are shown here. Some of the things you could evaluate are included. You will be able to think of others.

Evaluating designs

When you have finished your design you will evaluate the whole design. This is the **final evaluation**. Let's evaluate stir fry cooking.

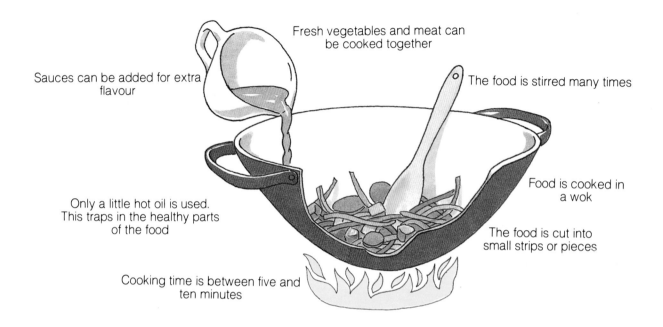

Sauces can be added for extra flavour

Fresh vegetables and meat can be cooked together

The food is stirred many times

Food is cooked in a wok

The food is cut into small strips or pieces

Only a little hot oil is used. This traps in the healthy parts of the food

Cooking time is between five and ten minutes

In the past a lot of time was spent preparing the family meal. Today families are very busy and have less time to prepare meals. We need to design ways to prepare meals that are simple and quick. The methods we use to cook must also give us healthy, tasty and filling meals.

For many centuries Chinese people have cooked food using the stir fry method. You can see how the food is cooked in the diagram above.

There are many other ways to make meals quickly. Here are some that you might think about.

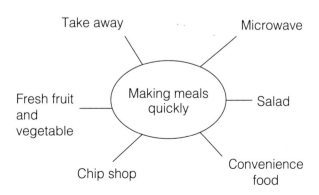

Take away

Microwave

Fresh fruit and vegetable

Making meals quickly

Salad

Chip shop

Convenience food

Activity

▶ Evaluate stir fry cooking.
Does it meet the needs of a busy family?

▶ What skills are needed?
Is it cheap to prepare?
Do you think Chinese meals are healthy?

▶ Have you ever eaten Chinese food?
Is it tasty?
Does it look appetising?
Is it filling?
If you haven't eaten Chinese food, interview someone who has to find out the information.

▶ A lot of the time is spent preparing food before it is cooked.
Design a system that might save preparation time.
You might prepare the food at a different time.

▶ Think of other ways to prepare meals quickly. The spider diagram will give you some ideas. Choose one method and evaluate it as you evaluated the stir fry method.
How do they compare?

You are part of a design team working on designs to save energy.

You are going to design and make a prototype model of a wind generator.

Activity

▶ Design and model your wind generator. You could use drawing, modelling tools and materials, modelling kits or a computer.

▶ Evaluate your design. Think about:
- cost
- size
- space
- use of energy
- materials and equipment used
- maintenance.

▶ Devise a test for your design. Does it work?

▶ What problems does your design have?

▶ How could the design be improved?

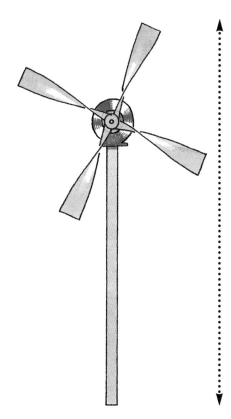

Actual height of model

30cm

There is a stretch of road that passes an old aged pensioners home. The bus stop is on the other side of the road. There is a problem. How can the pensioners get to the bus stop safely? A number of designs have been suggested.

- Placing a large bright warning sign on the road.
- Building a zebra crossing and having a traffic warden for three hours a day.
- Building a pedestrian underpass or walkway over the road.
- Putting in traffic lights.
- Moving the bus stop a mile down the road to where the road is quieter.

Activity

▶ Evaluate the designs from the point of view of:
(a) the pensioners
(b) the council building the design.

▶ Think about all the things they would take into account.

▶ Carry out a role play of a meeting between the council and pensioners.

Chapters 1-5 showed how you design and make things. You used the **design and technology process**. Here are some designs for artefacts, systems and environments. Each design starts at a different place.

Design an environment where people can eat
Start by finding out if there is a need and opportunity.

Identifying a need and opportunity
- Where is there an opportunity - home, school, industry, recreation, community?
- Find out information - interview, questionnaire, books.
- Identify:
  - what food people need
  - what type of environment they want
  - who will be eating the food.

↓

- Draw, write and model different designs.
- Choose one design.

↓

Plan and make the design.

↓

Evaluate the design.

Serving meals from boats. One idea for a new environment where people can eat.

Design a system to make learning fun
Start by thinking of ideas for designs.

Generating a design
- Identify the problem to be solved.
- Write the design brief, specifications and proposal.
- Identify the constraints.
- Develop ideas by: sketching; modelling; drawing; asking people's opinions; role play.
- Choose one of the designs.

↓

Plan and make the design.

↓

Evaluate the design.

↓

If the design is unsuccessful identify the needs and opportunities that were missed.

Activity and board games

Design a computer graphic to advertise in a shop window
Start by planning and making the graphic.

Planning and making
- Write a plan or production schedule.
- Decide on the order of tasks and the time for each.
- Choose your materials and equipment.
- Decide what skills are needed.
- Identify any problems.
- Decide on the method used to make the design.

Evaluate the design.

If the design is unsuccessful, identify the needs and opportunities that were missed.

- Draw, write and model different designs.
- Choose one design.

A video shop window

Design an artefact that you might find in a catalogue
Start by evaluating artefacts in catalogues.

Evaluating
- Does it: (a) meet a need; (b) look good; (c) work properly; (d) cost a lot?
- Is it safe?
- Was the method used to make it: (a) safe; (b) efficient; (c) costly?

If the design is unsuccessful, identify the needs and opportunities that were missed.

- Draw, write and model different designs.
- Choose one design.

Plan and make the design.

Artefacts in catalogues

Activity
► Choose one of the designs on these two pages.
Follow it through the design and technology process.
Remember to record your ideas at each stage.

Why do you collect information?

When did you last ask somebody for the right time? Have you ever asked a friend what they thought of your new clothes? Why do teachers take a register every morning?

Each person is finding out or collecting their own information. You will need to collect and record information when you are designing and making. The spider diagram gives you some reasons why. Finding out information is called **investigating** or doing **research**. There are many ways to do this. You will need to record all your results so that you can use them later.

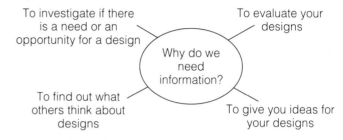

Activity

▶ In groups, discuss why you might find out:
  (a) how strong, stretchy or smooth materials are
  (b) which people like pop music
  (c) what people think about clothes.

Writing for information

You can collect information by writing to businesses, associations and people who can help your designs. It is important to remember a number of things.

• Keep a record of the person and the address the letter is sent to.
• State the address where the information is to be sent.
• State why you need the information.
• State exactly what information you need.
• State what you are going to do with it.
• Thank the person for their help.
• Sign and print your name.
• You should enclose a large stamped addressed envelope.

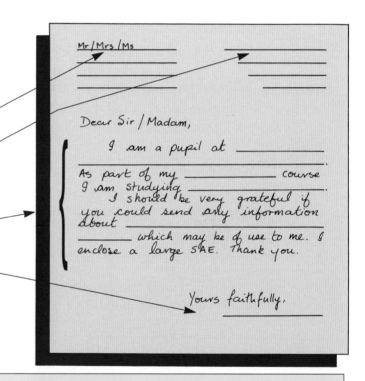

Activity

▶ Design and write a letter to ask for information about:
  (a) pet products
  (b) ski equipment
  (c) security or safety at home
  (d) travelling to Sweden by train
  (e) booking a room for a birthday party.

▶ Design a letter to arrange an interview with a designer of teenage clothes or a visit to a business.

▶ Choose one of the letters you have written. Re-write it using a word processing program on a computer.
  - Keep text over to the left.
  - Don't leave indent spaces at the start of new paragraphs.
  - Start paragraphs on a new line.
  How does it look different to the written letter?

Observing

You can collect information by looking and listening, studying how things work and watching what happens. You need to record your findings so that you can look at them later. The things you observe may help you to:
- find out if there are needs and opportunities for designing
- generate ideas for designs
- evaluate existing designs.

— Activity —

▶ Observe and record one of the following:
  (a) where people walk their dogs
  (b) how pupils use desks and chairs in school
  (c) a young child playing
  (d) taking food out of an oven.

▶ What ideas do you get for designs?

A technology student went to a local show. He observed many things and recorded them in three ways:
- a video
- a photograph
- notes.

A video camera can record what happens to play back later

You can also take a photograph of what you have seen

NOTES
I sat on a hill and watched the 'CITY FM' roadshow. The DJ played records to people. A dance competition was held. Five people danced on stage. The crowd chose the best dancer by clapping and shouting loudest.

There did not seem to be a lot of room to dance on stage.

— Activity —

▶ Look at the photograph and draw a sketch map of the scene.

▶ Make your own notes on the photograph.
What problems can you see?
Think about safety, pollution and the position of the stage.

▶ What designs might solve these problems?

▶ Why might the video give more information than the notes or the photograph?

Questionnaires

A questionnaire is a list of questions. It allows us to collect a great deal of information because it can be given to many people. When you are designing a questionnaire it is useful to follow a set of rules. They will help you. You can see these rules across the page.

You should also think carefully about the type of questions you will ask.
- **Closed questions**. A number of possible answers are given and you pick one.
- **Open questions**. They let someone say what they want in a few sentences.

Imagine you are writing a questionnaire to find out what people think about magazines. You will need to find out **facts**. Closed questions are best for this. You might want to know that a magazine reader is male. You can also find out people's **opinions**. The reader might think the magazine should have more pictures. Open questions are best for this but closed questions are also used.

Activity
▶ Write a closed question and an open question for a questionnaire to find out what old people need. You might think about food, clothing, transport or safety.
The questionnaire on page 51 will help you.

RULES FOR QUESTIONNAIRES

1. Think about what you are trying to find out - your aim.

2. Write questions in rough first. Make sure they are clear.

3. Try your questions out. Make changes if you have to.

4. Try typing your questionnaire. You could use a word processing computer program.

5. Make sure the person answering the questions knows who you are and what you are doing.

6. Make sure all answers are confidential. This means you will not tell others the name of the person who has given the answers.

7 Choose who will answer the questions. Send out your questionnaires by post or deliver them.

8. Decide how the questionnaire is to be filled in:
   - if you are doing it, get permission from your teacher and be polite when asking questions
   - if the person answering the questions is doing it, make sure they know what to do and where to return it.

9. Collect the questionnaires.

10. Write up your results and present them. You could use a computer database to store the data.

You can't ask everyone for answers. It is not possible to ask all runners in the London marathon if it was difficult. You should pick a group of people - a **sample**.

You must make sure that you pick enough people to get a good idea of everyone's views. You must also pick people who have actually run the marathon.

Activity
▶ In a group, discuss who you might ask about:
   (a) what you and your friends should do on Saturday
   (b) safety in your street
   (c) school meals
   (d) pollution in your area.
▶ How many people would you ask in each case?

Thousands of people run in the London Marathon. There are many different views and opinions.

MAGAZINE SURVEY

NO NAME - KEEP ANSWERS CONFIDENTIAL

KNOW WHAT YOU ARE TRYING TO FIND OUT

START WITH SIMPLE QUESTIONS

USE CLOSED QUESTIONS WITH FEW CHOICES, THEY ARE USUALLY BEST TO FIND OUT FACTS

SEX   male
      female

AGE under 10   18-25
    10-14   25-40
    15-18   over 40

ETHNIC ORIGIN

KNOW WHO IS ANSWERING THE QUESTIONS

European   Asian   Afro-Caribbean   Other

please state _____

Do you read magazines?   a lot
Tick one.   a little
                         never

Do you buy magazines?   a lot
Tick one.   a little
                        never

KEEP INSTRUCTIONS SIMPLE

Which type of magazine do you buy?

USE MULTI CHOICE QUESTIONS

sports
fashion
records
story
news
other (please state) _____

LEAVE DETAILED QUESTIONS UNTIL LATER

What do you think are the best parts of a magazine?

problem page
horoscope
puzzles
colour pin ups
articles about stars
other articles (please state) _____

CLOSED QUESTIONS CAN BE USED FOR OPINIONS

OPEN ENDED QUESTIONS ARE BEST FOR OPINIONS

What else would you like to see in a magazine?

_____
_____

Activity

▶ Try out the magazine survey above on a few friends.
  - You could type it out on a word processing program.
  - Use a database to store the data.
  - Study the data.
  - What information does it give you?
  - How could you improve the questionnaire?

▶ Design your own questionnaire for one of the following:
  (a) what TV programmes people would like to see more of and the most popular programmes
  (b) what music people over 20 like
  (c) what people feel about pollution in your area
  (d) how school books could be made more interesting
  (e) what your friends think of fast food outlets
  (f) accidents at home.
  - Try out the questionnaire.
  - Record the results.
  - What ideas for design do the results give you?

Market research

Have you ever seen someone standing with a clipboard asking questions? Have you seen figures showing that people prefer one product more than others? This is market research.

Businesses and government want a lot of information. Specialist agencies sometimes carry out **surveys** for other businesses - their clients. Many large businesses carry out their own surveys. They might want to find out who is buying their products or who might buy a new product. Sometimes they give away free samples of new products and ask for people's **opinions** about them.

BREAKFAST CEREALS 1987-1988

Share of market sales

KELLOGG	42%
WEETABIX	14%
NABISCO	8%
QUAKER	7%

A survey of breakfast cereal sales in 1987-88 showed Kellogg sold the most cereals

DECIDE ON THE AIM OF THE RESEARCH.
WOULD YOU BUY:
- AN ADDITIVE FREE BISCUIT?
- AN ALARM FOR YOUR BAG?

→

DESIGN A QUESTIONNAIRE
DECIDE WHO TO ASK

→

CARRY OUT THE RESEARCH
USE QUESTIONNAIRES
INTERVIEW PEOPLE WITH THEM

↓

FILL IN THE QUESTIONNAIRE DURING THE INTERVIEW

Carrying out market research

PRESENT THE RESULTS
WHAT DO THEY TELL YOU?
HOW CAN THEY BE USED?

←

COLLECT ALL THE QUESTIONNAIRES

←

GET PEOPLE TO TRY OUT FREE SAMPLES

Activity

► Why do you think:
(a) a business selling a new drink
(b) the Automobile Association or the RAC
might carry out research?
Write down all the information they would need to get.

► Find out what a government census is.
You can find the latest census in the library.
Why would the government want this information?

► Carry out a role play exercise in a group.
- Decide who are the researchers and who are the people being interviewed.
- Carry out a survey.
- What are you trying to find out?
- Record your results.
- Evaluate how the market research went.
- What improvements could you make?
- What information did you find?
- How could you use the information?

Interviews

You can find out many things by interviewing people. Interviews are 'chats' with people where you ask them for information or their opinions. You could interview your family or friends. You could also interview people who know about your designs. These are **experts**. You might want to interview a dentist to evaluate your new toothbrush design. Some experts charge for their time and advice. They are called **consultants**.

What things do you think your teachers are expert in?

Activity

▶ Who would you interview about:
  (a) how to manage a business
  (b) how to put on a buffet or party
  (c) how to decorate a theatre set
  (d) how to repair a car?

▶ Choose two teachers in your school.
  Make a list of the things they are expert in.

▶ Design an interview for local people to find out what they think about local shops and facilities.

Work time is important for many people. You must know what you want to ask before you contact them. A well designed interview will save time and give the best results. You should follow the 'Tips for interviewing'.

You must decide how to record your results. The spider diagram below may give you some ideas.

Activity

▶ Carry out a role play exercise.
  - Decide on a topic.
    It could be litter in your area or what people think about clothes or TV programmes.
  - Carry out interviews with your friends.
  - Record your results in two different ways.

▶ You have an idea about setting up a small business in school (tuck shop, mini-enterprise etc.).
  - Make a list of people you will need to ask about:
    (a) whether there is a need for it
    (b) whether you are allowed to do it
    (c) what you will need to start off
    (d) where to set up your stall.
  - Design a short interview for one of these people.
  - Carry out the interview.
  - What do your results show?

TIPS FOR INTERVIEWING

1. Decide who you are going to interview.

2. Decide what information you want to find out.

3. Plan the interview.
   Write down the questions you will ask.

4. Arrange the interview. Decide on a place and time. Get permission from your teacher. Arrange an appointment if you have to.

5. How are you going to record the information? Practice with any equipment first.

6. Do the interview. State who you are and what you are doing.

7. Be polite and keep the interview relaxed.

8. Don't waste time. Keep the interview short. Ask questions clearly.

9. Thank the person for the interview.

10. Write up your results after the interview.

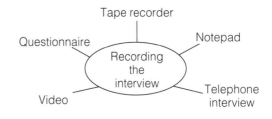

Doing experiments

You can test parts of your design as it is being developed. This will give you information that will help to improve your design.

You could **experiment** with the materials you are using in your design. When you experiment with materials you will have to think about what properties they have, such as:
- how strong they are
- how safe they are
- how they stand up to wear and tear.

If you are making a child's toy you might use materials that are:

Bendy · Stretchy · Strong · Twisty · Hard to scratch

1.KG

Sometimes new materials will be made. Here is an example. ICI developed BIOPOL, a new plastic. Experiments were carried out to see if it was suitable for making plastic products.

BIOPOL-ICI'S NEW PLASTIC

Biopol is a new type of plastic. It has many advantages over plastics which are used at present.

Bio-degradable

Biopol is as durable and water resistant as other plastics. Its advantage is that it degrades in compost and liquids, with or without oxygen. It can disappear completely in a matter of weeks in sewage. Biopol can be recycled from waste after consumers have finished with products.

The future

Biopol can be made into a wide range of products, such as bottles and fibres. In future it will be particularly useful in degradable products. These include all home and industrial products that find their way into soil, sewage systems, water systems and rubbish sites.

Source: adapted from *Steam*, ICI

You can also experiment with different ways of making something. You will need to ask:
- was your method quick enough
- did you need lots of skills
- did you waste material
- did you have the right quantity
- were you accurate
- does your method give the best results?

Activity

▶ Experiment with different methods to join together materials for a child's toy.
Think about the questions across the page.
Record your results.

▶ Experiment with different ways:
(a) to make bread
(b) of dyeing a tee-shirt
(c) of preserving wood.

A sensor 'senses' things that are happening. Sensors are used in many ways. Smoke alarms in the home and at work sense fumes. They set off a warning to people. Light sensors can tell you how much daylight there is.

Information can be collected using sensors. They are sometimes attached to a computer which stores and presents the data.

It is important to record all your results when experimenting. You could record them on a spreadsheet or database. You could then present the results as graphs.

Activity

▶ Discuss how sensors could be used:
(a) for safety in the home
(b) to investigate traffic congestion
(c) to evaluate acidity in water.

▶ In a group, design an experiment in your school using sensors.
- You could experiment with:
(a) the need for light or heat in your classroom
(b) the heat needed to boil vegetables
(c) the amount of water in a window garden
(d) the congestion in the corridor at different times of the day
(e) an idea of your own.
- Think about where you will place the sensors and the information you will need.
- Carry out the test.
- Record and present the results.

Making a sensing device using a logic board

CORRIDOR CONGESTION	Monday	Tuesday	Wednesday	Thursday	Friday
8.00 am - 9.00 am					
11.00 am -11.15 am					
12.30 pm -1.30 pm					

The results of your experiment could be recorded like this

Tests and trials

When you have planned and made your design you will test and trial it. This means getting people to try out your ideas or trying them yourself. You can then find out what people think and if the design works.

You will be able to evaluate the success of your design.
- Does it satisfy a need?
- Does it work?
- Does it solve a problem?
- Does it meet the design brief?

Businesses often carry out tests on products to see if they are safe and if they work well. Cookers, parachutes, drills, fires and waterproof clothing must all be tested to make sure that they are safe and that they do what they were made for.

New cars are given many tests. The law says that cars over 3 years old must be tested every year. If a car passes the test it is given a Ministry of Transport (MOT) certificate.

Testing motor cars

Activity

▶ Why do cars need to be tested?
What things would you test on a car?

▶ Design a test to see how long different foods last in a fridge. Carry out the test, then record and present your results.

▶ How would you test:
(a) a bag to carry shopping
(b) a pair of running shoes
(c) a microwave cooker
(d) a person's fitness
(e) an automatic camera?
Carry out the tests, then record and present your results.

Businesses also trial their products with the public before they sell them. They might:
- give away free samples of hair shampoo and chocolate bars
- show films to people before releasing them to cinemas
- set up exhibitions of paintings and sculptures.

They use questionnaires to gather information on the products and make final changes.

Activity

▶ Design tests for:
(a) finding out the price a new pencil will sell at
(b) opinions on a mural at the entrance to your school
(c) eating fish and rice instead of fish and chips
(d) the last video you saw.

▶ Carry out one of your tests.
Record and present your results.

Looking at an art exhibition

Tasting

Businesses sometimes use **tasting panels** to test their designs. Wine tasters and tea tasters are examples. You can carry out your own tasting by following the 'Rules for Tasting' across the page. When you have done your tasting you will need to record your results.

A group of 10 children were used to taste 3 drinks. They were:

> Drink A - chocolate
> Drink B - kiwi fruit
> Drink C - banana.

They placed the drinks in **rank order**. This means saying which was their first, second and third choice. Here are their results.

1st choice	2nd choice	3rd choice	Name
A	C	B	Jasmine
B	A	C	Joe
A	B	C	Hannatu
A	C	B	Intzar
C	B	A	Dave
B	C	A	Chen
A	B	C	Abnash
C	A	B	Alain
A	C	B	Natalie
A	C	B	Jean

Which drink did the class like most? You can add up or total the results. You can see that 6 students placed A as their first choice. An easy way to do this is to **tally** your results.

DRINK	1ST CHOICE	2ND CHOICE	3RD CHOICE
A	HHt I	II	II

The class results would be:

Drink	1st choice	2nd choice	3rd choice
A	6	2	2
B	2	3	5
C	2	5	3

You can use the results to say that the class liked drink A most, then drink C and then drink B.

1. Choose some people to taste the food or drink.

2. What do you want them to taste?

3. Give each plate or cup a letter. Sometimes you might not want the taster to see the food or drink. This is blind tasting.

4. Think about what people will use to describe the food or drink. They could test the smell, colour, taste, look, sound or feel.

5. Think about how they will record their opinions. An easy way is to ask the taster to give a number from 1-5, with 5 being the best. Here are Jasmine's results.

Drink	Smell	Taste	Colour	Texture	Total
A	4	5	4	3	16
B	2	2	1	1	6
C	2	3	3	3	11

Jasmine liked A then C then B

6. Carry out the tasting.

7. Make sure the taster drinks water before each food or drink. Make sure the spoon is clean.

8. Record and present your results. You could use a database or a spreadsheet. There are programs that will add up totals for you and give results.

Activity

▶ Design tastings for the following.
   (a) Can people tell the difference between butter and margarine?
   (b) Which food people would prefer as a side salad.
   (c) Invent a new flavour for a drink. Test it against other drinks.

▶ Design your own tasting panel. Decide what to test. Record and present your results.

Which? magazine

Sometimes you will not be able to carry out your own research.
- There may not be enough time.
- Tests may be complicated or dangerous.
- The information may be from the past, different countries or other parts of your own country.

You may have to look for information in books, magazines, papers and databases.

Which? magazine is published by the Consumers' Association. It comes out every month. *Which?* magazine compares different products and presents information about them.

How does it find out the information? It sends questionnaires to makers of the products it is testing and to shops. It can find out where these things are sold and their price.

It also buys products from shops and tests them. Food and drink are tested by tasting panels. Televisions and videos are tested in a laboratory.

Here is a *Which?* magazine report on washing powder.

THE BRANDS WE TESTED

Brand	Sizes available	Cost for 500ml size [1] (p)	Number of plates washed per 5ml squirt	Number of plates washed for 50p
Ark	500ml, 1 litre	72	©©	©
▶ Asda	500ml, 1 litre, 2 litres	39	©©	©©©
▶ Asda Concentrated	500ml	53	©©©	©©©©
▶ Boots	750ml, 5 litres	55 (750ml)	©©	©©©
▶ Boots Concentrated	1 litre	101 (1 litre)	©©©	©©©©
▶ Co-op	500ml, 1litre	40	©©	©©©
▶ Co-op Concentrated	500ml, 1 litre	55	©©©	©©©
Ecover	500ml, 1 litre, 5 litres	65	©	©
▶ Fairy	500ml, 1 litre	59	©©©©	©©©©©
▶ Gateway Diamond	1 litre	63 (1 litre)	©©	©©©
▶ Gateway Diamond Concentrated	500ml	54	©©©	©©©©
▶ Morning Fresh	500ml, 1 litre	53	©©©	©©©
▶ Persil	500ml, 1 litre	59	©©©	©©©
▶ Safeway	500ml, 1 litre	43	©©	©©©
▶ Safeway Concentrated	500ml, 1 litre	53	©©©	©©©
▶ Sainsbury's	500ml, 1 litre	39	©©	©©©
Sainsbury's Greencare	1 litre	99 (1 litre)	©©	©©
▶ Sainsbury's Super Concentrated	500ml, 1 litre	53	©©©	©©©©
▶ Sqezy	500ml	43	©©	©©©
St Michael Harvest Concentrated	750ml	125 (750ml)	©©©	©©
▶ Sunlight	500ml, 1 litre	58	©©©	©©©
▶ Tesco	750ml	50 (750ml)	©©	©©©©
Tesco Cares [2]	1 litre	99 (1 litre)	©©	©©
▶ Waitrose Mild	500ml, 1 litre	39	©©	©©©
▶ Waitrose Concentrated	500ml, 1 litre	53	©©©	©©©©

© = washed up to 16 plates
©© = washed between 17 and 26 plates
©©© = washed between 27 and 36 plates
©©©© = washed between 37 and 47 plates

© = washed up to 1,500 plates
©© = washed up to 2,400 plates
©©© = washed up to 2,900 plates
©©©© = washed up to 3,400 plates
©©©©© = washed up to 3,900 plates

[1] The price given is for a 500ml size, if available, and is based on prices we found in our shopping survey. Where a 500ml size isn't sold, we've given the price for the nearest size available (and have shown this size in brackets)
[2] Due to be repackaged as Tesco Greenchoice in July

Source: *Which?* July 1991

Activity

▶ Look at the results of the *Which?* magazine survey. Form a group and discuss which brand you think is:
(a) the best
(b) the worst.
Write down the reasons for your choices.

▶ How could information from the survey on washing powder be useful for:
(a) a restaurant owner
(b) a shopkeeper
(c) someone concerned about the environment?

▶ Carry out your own survey.
You will not be able to carry out the research in as much detail as *Which?*.
Choose products that are already in your house.
- Find a product which you and your friends all have at home.
- Note the different brands.
- Make a list of the things you will find out. You could record the price, features, size of screen and picture quality of a TV. You could find out about computer games, clothing or snacks.
- Use a key for how good things are:

Good ▢ ◪ ▨ ◪ ■ Poor

- Record and present your results.

Databases

Databases are collections of information which are stored away for you to use. Today much of the information is stored on computer or computer disk.

You might be able to find:
- weather maps
- nutritional information on food
- useful addresses to write to for information, such as the Advertising Association.

Teletext information can be found on Ceefax and Oracle. These are databases which can be found on some television sets. They store a large amount of information. This includes TV programmes, sports results, travel news and reviews of events.

There are many large databases that can be used by a telephone linked to a computer. These include NERIS, an educational database, and PAL, a travel agents' booking database.

Your library will have a number of databases. These contain information about books. Some libraries will still have filing systems on cards. Most will use a **microfiche**.

Many databases are now on computers or software. But people still use telephone directories and the *Yellow Pages*.

You can design your own database. There are many software packages to help you. You can use it to record the results of your surveys.

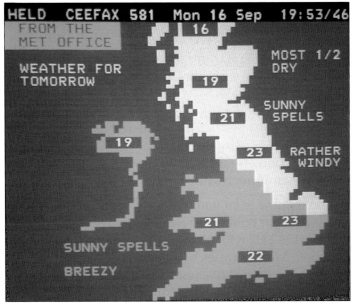
Ceefax information

Yellow pages

▭ **Activity** ▭

▶ Look at the databases on this page. What ideas do you get for designs? Write or draw your designs.

▶ Use a database at school or at home to find out about:
  (a) the dietary fibre in food
  (b) important news items
  (c) travel times and services
  (d) what is on in your local area.
Use the information to develop ideas for designs.
You could:
- plan a holiday or visit
- design a front page of a newspaper
- design a meal for an athlete that is low in sugar.

Written information

Most of the books and magazines you can use will be in the local library or the library at school.

Books are divided into:

- **fiction** - books which are not based on facts such as story books
- **non-fiction** - books with factual information such as this one.

You will know from your work on databases that books are recorded on a microfiche. This will tell you where to find the book. Most libraries have subject headings written above non-fiction books. You could also ask the librarian.

When you have found your book you will need to know where to turn. This is shown across the page.

Some pages of books have a large number of words. You will need to **scan** or **skim** the page for information. You could:

- read through the page first
- make short notes
- underline important words.

Here is a page from a history book about Rome titled 'A day at the races'. Your notes could look like these below.

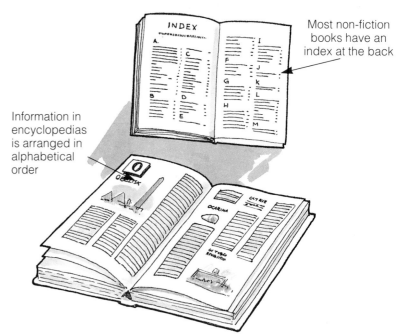

Most non-fiction books have an index at the back

Information in encyclopedias is arranged in alphabetical order

Finding information in books

NOTES
1. Romans held <u>races</u> for entertainment.
2. Charioteers raced in <u>teams</u>.

Activity

▶ Scan the page titled 'A day at the races'.

▶ Make short notes.

▶ Tell a friend about Roman races from your notes.

▶ Use the information to design a simple board game.

A day at the races

Charioteers raced in teams - the Greens, Blues, Whites or Reds. Throughout the Empire, charioteers would race for one of these teams. Supporters were loyal to their favourite colour, just as people today are loyal to their favourite football team. In AD 390, supporters rioted after their favourite charioteer was put into prison!

Successful charioteers were the popular heroes of their day.

Although many were born slaves, they could win their freedom and great wealth at the races. Gambling was very popular in the Roman world. This was one reason for the popularity of chariot races. Spectators would place bets on their favourite chariots.

Source A

I beg you demon, whoever you are, from this hour, from this day, from this moment, torture the horses of the Greens and Whites. Kill them! Make sure that the charioteers Clarus and Felix crash! Leave no breath in them! And then, let the Red team win.

Curse written on a lead tablet found in Africa

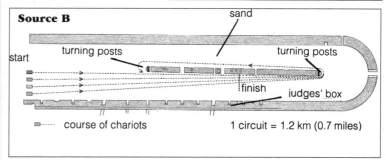

Source B

start

turning posts

sand

turning posts

finish

judges' box

course of chariots

1 circuit = 1.2 km (0.7 miles)

Plan of a chariot race

You can also use written information on leaflets to help with your designs.

Activity

► You are designing a theme park.
It could be about Romans or any idea of your own.
- Use the library to find books on the subject.
- Use the indexes to help you.
- Read about your ideas in an encyclopedia.
- Make notes.
- Ask other people about their visits to theme parks.
- Look at advertisements for theme parks and shows.

► Design your theme park.
Draw your design.
Think about the rides, amusements and shops that you will plan and make.

► Choose one idea for a ride.
Draw and model your design.
Evaluate it.
- Test if your design works.
- Is it safe?
- Ask others for their opinions.

Leaflets for theme parks

You must be careful when using other people's information. Remember that facts are things that can be tested. A school report that said 15 pupils were absent could be tested. We say this is **objective** information.

Other information is about people's opinions. A report on litter in your area may say that a bottle bank should be placed on every main road. We say this information is **subjective**. It is the opinion of the writer. It is based on what she thinks is important.

Activity

► Which of the statements across the page are facts and which are opinions?

► Choose a page of any book or magazine. In a group, discuss which statements are facts and which are opinions on the page.

'The height of a door is 2 metres.'

'I think most people prefer red to blue.'

'This meal would be better if it had pasta rather than chips.'

'The volume of traffic has been measured at 10 cars every minute.'

'The length of the sleeves are 2 mm longer than the pattern.'

'The manager believes more people would visit his shop if it was in the high street.'

Pictures and graphs

Magazines, catalogues, leaflets, manuals and newspapers contain lots of pictures. They will give you ideas for your own designs.

They will also give you information about how designs are made, the materials that are used and perhaps even the cost.

A group of students were designing and making structures. They found the pictures across the page.

Childrens' toys using structures

Activity

▶ Where might you find the pictures across the page?

▶ Use the information in the photograph of toys to design a toy with a frame.
Draw and model your design.

▶ What ideas for designs using glass walls or a glass roof do you get from the conservatories in the advertisement?
Draw and model your ideas.

▶ Use magazines, newspapers, catalogues and manuals to collect information about one of the following:
- advertising styles
- house designs
- healthy eating
- hygiene
- sportswear
- the cost of convenience and health food.
Write a design brief from your information.

UPVC AND HARDWOOD CONSERVATORIES
VICTORIAN - EDWARDIAN - GEORGIAN - REGENCY
ELIZABETHAN

An advertisement for conservatories

You can find information from charts, graphs, tables and figures.

Activity

▶ Look at the information in the pie chart.
- What does it tell a designer of:
(a) sports equipment
(b) comics?
- What does it tell schools about the time spent on homework?

▶ In a group, discuss how children could be encouraged to spend more time on homework.
Record and present your results.

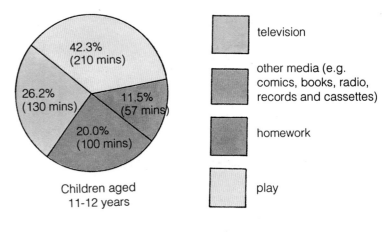

42.3% (210 mins)

26.2% (130 mins)

11.5% (57 mins)

20.0% (100 mins)

Children aged 11-12 years

television

other media (e.g. comics, books, radio, records and cassettes)

homework

play

Research from the USA. It shows the amount of time children spend on different activities in a normal day.

Case studies

Case studies give detailed information about something or somebody. They will give you ideas for designs to satisfy people's needs.

Hannah Green Aged 13

Now that I am in my teens I am aware I could get spots and my skin and hair could get greasy. I have decided to try and eat less convenience food for my lunch if I can. I like to eat chocolate after my lunch because it seems to give me energy for the afternoon. I would like to eat something else to give me energy.

Activity

▶ Identify the needs of Hannah Green and Brookdale Ltd.

▶ Design things that could satisfy their needs.

▶ Draw and write your designs.

▶ Evaluate your designs. Did they satisfy the needs you identified?

Brookdale Limited

Businessman Kevin Potts set up in business 6 months ago. He makes leaflets and advertising brochures. Brookdale has expanded quickly. They now find it difficult to keep a record of their customers. Kevin used to know them all, but now there are too many. They are also running out of floor space to store the leaflets.

You can write your own case studies. If you were collecting information on a business you could use the methods across the page. When writing a case study:

THINK ABOUT YOUR AIM. WHAT ARE YOU TRYING TO FIND OUT?
↓
DECIDE HOW TO GET THE INFORMATION
↓
GET PERMISSION TO ASK FOR THE INFORMATION
↓
CARRY OUT THE RESEARCH AND RECORD THE INFORMATION
↓
STORE THE INFORMATION SAFELY SO NO ONE ELSE CAN SEE IT
↓
DECIDE WHICH INFORMATION IS USEFUL AND WHICH IS NOT
↓
WHAT IDEAS FOR DESIGN DO YOU GET?

Activity

▶ What information would you find out from a business if:
  (a) a new piece of machinery was going to be designed
  (b) the workers' eating environment was going to be redesigned?

▶ Write your own case study on one of the following:
  (a) someone you know well
  (b) a local shop
  (c) an elderly or handicapped person.
  What ideas for designs do you get?

Graphs, charts and tables

You will collect a lot of facts and figures from your research and investigations. We call this **data**. You need to present the data clearly. This will make it easier to understand.

Carlo and Rahila are two technology students. They decided to investigate the items lost in school by their class over a number of weeks. How did they present their results?
- As a **table**.
- As a **bar chart**.
- As a **pie chart**.
Some were drawn by hand. Others were drawn on a home computer.

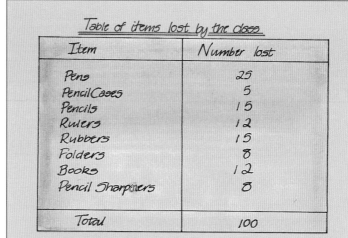

Table of items lost by the class

Item	Number lost
Pens	25
Pencil Cases	5
Pencils	15
Rulers	12
Rubbers	15
Folders	8
Books	12
Pencil Sharpeners	8
Total	100

Tables can show figures about the items that were lost.

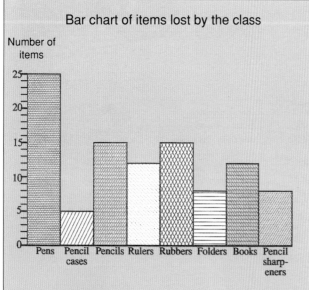

Bar chart of items lost by the class

Bar charts are used to show the number of times something happens. The height of a bar tells you this. The number or quantity is always on the vertical axis.

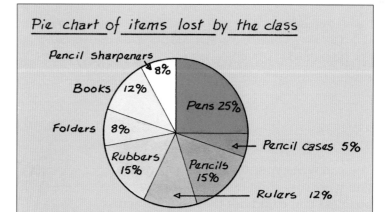

Pie chart of items lost by the class

A pie chart is a way of showing how a total or whole is divided into sectors or parts. The total number of items is drawn as a whole circle.

How do you draw the sector for the number of pens that were lost? It is useful to know what percentage of the total items lost were pens. 25 pens were lost out of 100. You can write:

$$\tfrac{25}{100} \times 100 = 25\%.$$

You can now work out the angle for the sector in the pie chart. You have to work out 25% of 360° = 90°.

Activity

Look at the ways that Carlo and Rahila presented the data.

▶ You want to find out which item was lost most often. Which method shows this most clearly?

▶ Think of different ways to arrange the order of the items in the bar chart above.
Re-draw the bar chart.
Is it easier to understand?

▶ Draw a pie chart from the data on the composition of wheat below.

Composition of wheat	
Moisture	14 %
Carbohydrate	70 %
Protein	13 %
Fat	1.5%
Minerals	1.5%

The investigation into lost items on the opposite page did not include any research on **time**.

When you look at different times you use a **line graph**. Time is placed on the horizontal axis. Quantity is placed on the vertical axis.

Activity

▶ What things could you record in your school using a line graph?

▶ Draw a line graph for the data below.

Temperature in Orlando, Florida (°F)	82	87	89	90	90	88	83	76
Month	APR	MAY	JUN	JUL	AUG	SEP	OCT	NOV

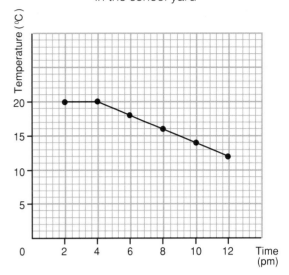

Temperature range on July 15 between 2pm and 12pm in the school yard

You will find many interesting examples of graphs, charts and tables in magazines. With a little imagination you can turn your own presentations into eye catching displays. Here are some examples.

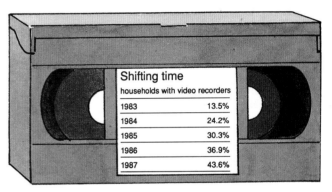

Shifting time
households with video recorders

1983	13.5%
1984	24.2%
1985	30.3%
1986	36.9%
1987	43.6%

Activity

▶ What methods of presentation are illustrated across the page?

▶ What information are the charts and tables giving you?
How could you use it to:
(a) identify a need
(b) generate a design idea
(c) evaluate a design?

▶ Design an eye catching chart for the data on energy below.

Energy used during activity

Activity	Energy used (kJ)
Sleeping	250
Reading	300
Walking	750
Cycling	1500
Swimming	1700
Running	2800

▶ Design interesting displays for the data on the opposite page.

Eating habits of schoolchildren (percentage eating foods daily)

Source: Nutrition Unit of the DHSS

Fish/fish fingers 64% 67%

Vegetables 94% 95%

Boys (aged 14/15)
Girls

71% 56% Baked beans

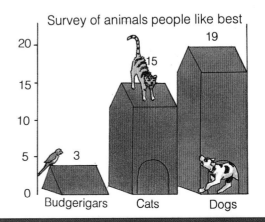

Survey of animals people like best

Budgerigars 3
Cats 15
Dogs 19

Using drawings, descriptions and photographs

You will find many other ways to present information. You could experiment with different methods. Which do people find easiest to understand?

You could:
- present the results of your research as drawings or opinions
- present your design ideas using magazine or newspaper cuttings
- present your evaluation as opinions or descriptions.

Across the page are some examples. It is important to check with your teacher whether you have to ask permission to use other people's material. Always say where you found the information.

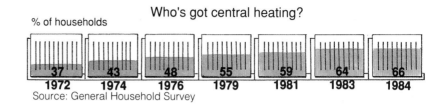

Who's got central heating?

% of households

37	43	48	55	59	64	66
1972	1974	1976	1979	1981	1983	1984

Source: General Household Survey

Source: Black Country Development Corporation

Activity

▶ Carry out research into the eating habits of your class.
Present the results as an interesting drawing.

▶ Look at the presentation of the office building. Why do you think the student says the building is a good shape for collecting the sun's energy?

▶ Collect drawings of office buildings. Design and draw your own office building.

▶ Present an idea for a design using a pyramid shape.
Ask for people's opinions.
Present your results.

Here is an artist's impression of a design for office buildings on a new industrial estate. The design is based on a pyramid. If the glass was used to collect the sun's energy for solar power then the design of the building would be very useful.

Computer storage and retrieval

Computers can store and present information in different ways.

You have been given the task of investigating the following things:
- whether girls prefer different food to boys
- light levels in your school at different times of the day
- the breaking strengths of different materials.

Activity

▶ Decide how to collect the data for one of the tasks.

▶ Record the results on a database or spreadsheet.

▶ Use a computer to present the results in different ways. Which way presents them most clearly?
You might have a computer program that can present the data as different types of graph.

▶ What ideas for designs do you get from your graphs, charts and tables?

Symbols

Symbols are a short and simple way of giving information. They allow the presenter to give lots of information in a small space.

If you use symbols in a diagram you must also give a key so that people will know what the symbols mean.

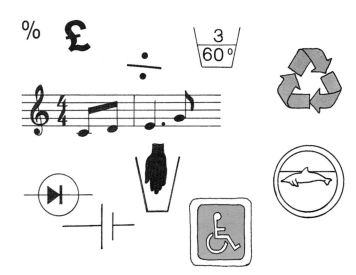

Activity

▶ What do the symbols opposite mean?

▶ Draw a plan of your school, home or local environment. The map below may help you.
  - Design your own symbols to show features on the map.
  - Draw a key for the map.
  - Ask someone to use your map.
  - Evaluate how effective it was.

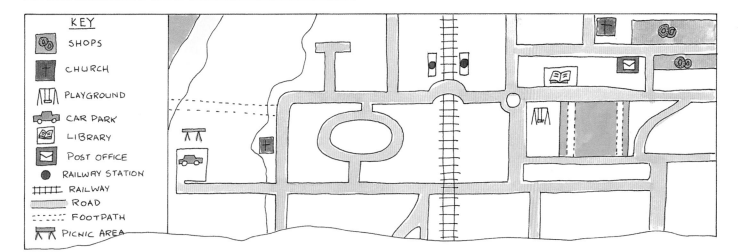

Many signs and symbols are used to communicate instructions.

Activity

▶ What do the symbols opposite communicate?

▶ Which ones communicate warnings? How do you know?

▶ Design a symbol to communicate one of the following:
  (a) a hazard
  (b) directions
  (c) a stopping point on a road
  (d) environmental information
  (e) health information.

Presentations and displays

Presentations are a good way to show off your ideas to people. It is important when making a presentation to decide:
- what information you are trying to get across
- the audience you want to see the presentation
- the way in which the information is presented.

After you have presented your design information you could ask for comments. These will help you to evaluate your work and improve your designs. If you are a member of the audience, ask questions. You may be able to use what you find out in your own designs.

In order to gather information for your presentation you should keep a **portfolio**. This is a file containing:
- the results of your research
- your design brief and design proposals
- your design ideas and drawings
- your plans
- your evaluation.

Activity

▶ Look at the presentation being given below by the two students.
  - What information are they presenting?
  - Write down the ways in which the information is being presented.
  - What type of audience are they talking to?

▶ As a group make a short presentation on one of the following:
  (a) helping people in need
  (b) your hobby
  (c) a design for a mobile filing cabinet
  (d) hygiene in the kitchen.
  Use the 'Tips for Presentations' on page 69 to help you.

▶ Evaluate your presentation from the question above.
  How could you improve it next time?

TIPS FOR PRESENTATIONS

Think about the following things.

1. What is your aim? What information are you trying to present?
2. Will you give the presentation as a group or on your own? If more than one person is giving it you must make sure everyone knows their job.
3. Who will be your audience?
4. When you give a short talk, will you read from notes?
5. What equipment will you need? Will you use an overhead projector, a slide projector or a cassette recorder?
6. How will you present the information? Will you use handouts or a model? You may need to prepare handouts before the presentation. You could use a computer word processing program. You could type the handout and then photocopy it or run it off.
7. How long will the presentation be? Try to keep it short and interesting.
8. Are you going to allow comments and questions at the end? What will you do with this information?

You could present your design information by setting up a **display**. You could put it in the classroom or the corridor. Try to make your display as colourful and interesting as you can. Use diagrams, models and photographs as well as things you have written.

When planning your display you should think about the things in the spider diagram below.

You could leave a questionnaire in a box for people to answer. This will give you information about your design and your display.

An industrial display

A school display

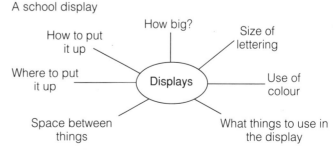

Activity

▶ What things are being used to display the information in the photographs?

▶ In a group, discuss and record the best and the worst things about the displays in the photographs.

▶ Plan a display for one of the following:
   (a) modern fabrics
   (b) safety when using equipment
   (c) the influence of foreign food on the British diet
   (d) school sports
   (e) unusual building structures.
   - Write down what you would use in your display.
   - Draw a rough sketch to show how the display would look.

▶ Write a questionnaire to help you evaluate your display in the question above.
   Ask people to fill it in.
   What do the results tell you?

Getting ideas from graphs and tables

Your research will give you a great deal of **data**. You will present some of it as a graph, a chart or a table. You will then need to **interpret** the information - find out what it is telling you. This will give you ideas for designs.

Ingrid carried out a survey into the variety of school meals. She presented her results as a bar chart. Then she interpreted them.

RESEARCH INTO SCHOOL MEALS

GENERATE IDEAS FOR DESIGN

INTERPRETING THE RESULTS

NUMBER OF PEOPLE QUESTIONED

NOT ENOUGH VARIETY / ENOUGH VARIETY

I asked 80 pupils about the variety of school meals. 60 said there was not enough variety and 20 said there was.
The results show that there might be a need for more variety in school meals.

TAGLIATELLI + GARLIC BREAD

CURRY + PITTA BREAD

Hold an 'Italian' or 'Indian' day at school. Design meals from other countries on the menu. Serve these meals at lunchtime.

Sometimes it is easier to understand the results of your research if they are rearranged. One way to do this is to put the data in order. This is called **sequencing**. The most popular is placed on top. The second most popular is placed below it. This carries on until the least popular is placed at the bottom.

100 people were asked which features they liked best in teenage magazines. The results were then sequenced. They are shown in the table across the page.

The most popular features in teenage magazines

Feature	Number of people
Pictures of pop stars	20
Problem pages	20
Fashion features	15
Pop star features	14
Horoscopes	13
Puzzles	9
Adverts	6
Environment features	2
Social features	1
Total	100

Looking for links and patterns

When you are interpreting your results you could look for links and patterns. They show how one thing can affect another. You might find a link between people's age and the music they like.

Across the page are charts and graphs showing the results of:
- a survey into the music that 14-16 year olds like in a school
- an experiment by scientists to show how springs stretch as weights are added.

Activity

▶ What patterns can you see in the results of the music survey? (You could sequence the data.)

▶ Carry out your own research into the music that 12-13 year olds like.
  - Record and present your results.
  - Is there a link between your results and the results of the survey opposite?
  - How might this information help the music industry?

▶ Use the information from the research on music to design a record promotion.
  You could:
  (a) draw an advert, poster or record sleeve
  (b) record a jingle on cassette
  (c) make a video.

▶ What link is there between mass and stretch in the line graph? How might this help in the design of:
  (a) a weighing machine
  (b) a fitness tester
  (c) a tape measure?

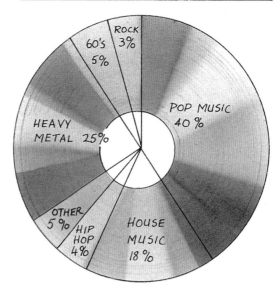

MUSIC SURVEY FOR 14 - 16 YEAR OLDS

Line graph showing the distance a spring stretches at different weights

Some students carried out research into items that were lost at school. Here are their results. They were researching:
- the need for school insurance
- safer designs for school bags.

Activity

▶ Which bags are the most and the least popular?

▶ Is there a link between the type of bag and the items lost?

▶ Design a bag to keep school things safe.
  Model your design using paper, card or clay.

▶ Design your own insurance scheme.
  - How much will you charge each pupil?
  - How much will you pay out for each item lost?
  - Work out whether you will make a profit or not?
  - How will your scheme have to be changed if it does not make a profit?

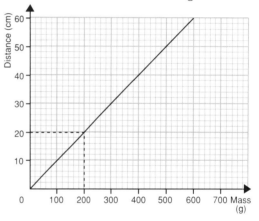

Survey of 20 people

People asked	Have you lost anything?	Type of bag	What has been lost?
1	Yes		Pen
2	No	Shoulder	—
3	Yes	Sports	Pencil Case
4	Yes	Plastic	Money
5	Yes	Sports	Pencil Case
6	No	Shoulder	
7	No	Sports	
8	Yes	Shoulder	Gloves
9	No	Plastic	—
10	Yes	Zip up	Money
11	No	Zip up	
12	Yes	Plastic	Tipp-Ex
13	Yes	Zip up	Soccer Ball
14	No	Sports	
15	No	RuckSack	—
16	Yes	Plastic	Football Boots
17	No	Sports	—
18	Yes	Plastic	Biscuits
19	No	Zip up	—
20	No	Sports	
		Ruck Sack	

Ideas from written information and opinions

Not all information will come as numbers or graphs. You could look through written work or notes to get ideas for your designs.

Activity

▶ Look at the information on washing-up tips.
  - What ideas do you get for:
    (a) a poster or leaflet on hygienic washing
    (b) equipment to use when washing-up
    (c) a washing-up liquid?
  - Choose one of the above or any of your own ideas.
  - Write or draw your design.

▶ How could you use the information on washing-up to evaluate washing at home and in a restaurant?

WASHING-UP TIPS

The liquid is only part of the key to effective washing-up. Here we give our tips to make the most of your chosen brand:
- Use water as hot as your hands can bear, or use rubber or PVC gloves.
- Generate a good amount of foam, either by swishing your hand or by adding the washing-up liquid while the water is running into the bowl - foam helps to prevent dirt from being redeposited on to dishes as you take them out of the water.
- Rinse well. In our survey just over a third of members said they always rinse dishes after washing them. Although it is unlikely that there is any health risk from eating off unrinsed plates, it would seem sensible, for gastronomic reasons, to rinse plates - to remove any dirt or perfume.
- If there is space, leave to drain dry - generally more hygienic than using a tea towel.

Source: *Which?*, July 1991

A group of girls did some research into how PE teachers felt about them playing football. They recorded the interviews. Then they wrote down some comments.

Activity

▶ What does each teacher think about girls playing football?

▶ What patterns can you see in the information?

▶ What ideas for design does it give you?

Mrs Parker said that she wouldn't give us her support because she doesn't think that it is healthy for girls. For example, when boys do a chest pass it doesn't hurt. But if girls do a chest pass or get a hard kick it can cause problems.

Ms Mendez. 'Some girls adapt themselves more to sport than boys and take it more seriously. Girls are discriminated against in sport as they are thought to be weaklings and vulnerable in competitive male sports. There should be more opportunities for girls in sports.'

Mr Ahmed. He said that teachers haven't got the time to teach us girls. Lads have been playing since they were about 6 and they have more experience, but we would have to learn from scratch. Also boys are stronger and so they are more suited to these sports than girls.

Mr Taylor. 'Girls do play football as well as most other boys sports. Although there are a few, there are not that many.'

Inventions

Coming up with completely new designs is not as easy as it seems. Ideas that no-one else has thought about are rare. People who think up original ideas are **inventors**. They often get a **patent** for their ideas. This means that nobody else can use the idea without the inventor's permission.

Many new designs are **adaptations**. This means someone has changed the original design to fit a new situation.

Cats eyes. Designed in 1934 by Percy Shaw. They allow motorists to see the middle of the road.

The Polaroid camera. It was designed in 1947 by Edwin Lord. Pictures can be taken and photographs are produced by the camera.

Activity

► Which of the designs in the photos has failed?
  Discuss why you think it failed.
  How could you adapt it?

► Try to design a new type of:
  (a) drink
  (b) game.
  Is your drink or game new, or an adaptation?

► How could you adapt:
  (a) shoes for comfort
  (b) roads for safety?

A swimming machine from 1880

Brainstorming

This is a well tested way to get new ideas for designs. One idea or word is put down on paper. You then have to think of as many new ideas as you can. You can work on your own or in a group.

Activity

► Hold a brainstorming session on hobbies.
  - The spider diagrams across the page will give you some ideas.
  - Set a time limit.
    It could be short, say five minutes, or longer, say fifteen minutes.
  - Write down as many ideas as you can.
    It does not matter if they are silly.

► Now try brainstorming these ideas:
  (a) making changes in school
  (b) improving a housing estate.

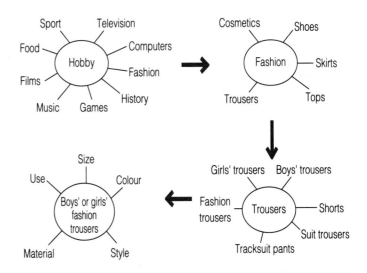

Brainstorming ideas about hobbies

Considering all features

Designs have many different features. You can make a list of all the features of the design. Then try changing one or two. You may find your designs satisfy different needs. You might list all the features under the headings 'good' and 'bad'. You could then pick out the features that are most interesting.

Activity

▶ How has the Mars Bar in the photograph been changed?
  - Try changing the fillings of different foods.
  - What will your designs be like?
  - What new needs will they satisfy?
  - Will others like them?

▶ Look at the chair opposite.
  - List all of its features.
  - Change some of them to make the chair:
    (a) more comfortable
    (b) suitable for a young child
    (c) match the decor of your front room.
  - Draw your new designs.

▶ Discuss and write down all the good, bad and interesting points of:
  (a) brown paper bags
  (b) plastic packaging
  They have been started for you across the page.

▶ Write all the good, bad and interesting points of:
  (a) school uniform
  (b) DIY furniture
  (c) shopping centres
  (d) cream cakes.

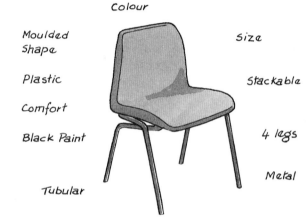

Colour
Moulded Shape
Size
Plastic
Stackable
Comfort
Black Paint
4 legs
Metal
Tubular

BROWN PAPER BAGS		
Pluses	Minuses	Interesting bits
Degrades	Rips when wet	Recyclable

PLASTIC PACKAGING		
Pluses	Minuses	Interesting bits
Cheap	Does not rot	Transparent

Alternatives

There are many different ways to do something. You can get ideas for your designs and how to make them by thinking about alternatives.

Activity

▶ Compare:
  (a) disposable with non-disposable plates and cutlery
  (b) a white board with a blackboard to show information.
  In each case say which you think is best.
  Give reasons for your answers.

▶ What other alternatives can you think of for:
  (a) washing-up
  (b) showing information?

An alternative to washing-up?

What would happen if . . . ?

What would happen if there was no electricity in your house? You would have to design equipment that worked without electricity.

Here are some interesting ideas for equipment that does not use electricity.

Activity

▶ Think of a design for a machine that does not use electricity.
Draw or model your design.

▶ Choose one of these situations.
(a) What if there were no cars, buses or lorries?
(b) What if there was no police force?
(c) What if there was a sudden food shortage?
(d) What if all fields were covered in buildings?
- What would it be like?
- What problems would you have to solve?
- Write or draw designs to solve the problems.

A washing machine (1884) turned by hand.

A clockwork talking machine (1903). It was thought the discs could be made from chocolate!

A teamaker (1902) made up of an alarm clock, a spirit lamp and a device to tip the kettle.

Lateral thinking

You can get ideas for designs by looking at things in different ways. This is called lateral thinking. The idea was first used by an American, Edward De Bono.

How many times have you heard people say 'We always do it this way'? Why not try the opposite? This is lateral thinking. Why not use square wheels instead of round ones? Why not have edible toothpaste?

Activity

▶ Think of all the ways that square wheels could be useful.

▶ When might you use:
(a) a polystyrene mallet instead of a wooden one
(b) a paper ruler rather than a plastic one?

▶ Try your own lateral thinking.
- Think of an artefact, system or environment at home.
- You could use an item of clothing such as pyjamas, a meal such as breakfast cereal or a room such as a garage.
- How could it be different?

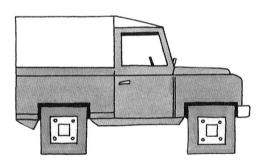

Round wheels changed to square wheels
(useful on slippery surfaces)

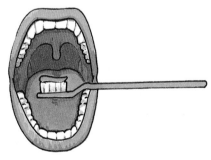

Edible toothpaste
(to get people to clean their teeth)

Finishing on time

You have to get to school on time. If you planned to arrive at 3.00pm you would miss your lessons. Newspapers must be out on time. Imagine a newspaper with today's stories coming out next week. It would not have been planned very well. No one would buy it. Businesses work to **deadlines**. A deadline is the time by which a job must be finished.

When you are designing and making you must decide how long you will take. If you finish on time your design will be successful.

Activity

▶ What deadlines must be met across the page?

▶ Make a list of all the deadlines you work to.

▶ What might happen if:
(a) you
(b) a business
did not meet deadlines?

▶ Why do businesses say 'time is money'?

DEADLINES

'You must get your homework in on time.'

'You can stay out until 10 pm.'

'The game starts at 3.30 pm.'

'The train leaves at 9.00 am.'

RETURN BY 10 SEPT 1992 TO HEYWOOD LIBRARY

Cook for 10 minutes.

'The meeting is in one hour.'

BUS TIMETABLE

    9.06

    10.06

    11.06

When planning and making your design you should try to be **efficient**. This means making the best use of the time you have. There may be ways to make your design more quickly. You will then become more efficient.

Activity

▶ Make a paper spiral or a paper model, or carry out a simple task such as preparing fruit or vegetables.
Time how long it takes.

▶ Now give yourself a deadline.
- Try to do the task within the deadline.
- Think of three ways to do the task more quickly.
Try them out.

▶ How does working to a deadline affect:
(a) how well a design is made
(b) how many items you can make?

▶ What constraints are there in doing the task?
How do they affect the deadline?

Organising tasks

Anything that you do is made up of a number of smaller tasks. Some are more important than others. If time is short you may have to leave out some of these tasks. To do this you must **prioritise** them - decide which are the most important.

You will also need to think about the order in which you will carry out the tasks. Which has to be done first? What comes next? We call this **sequencing** the tasks.

It might be possible to do two tasks together. This will save time.

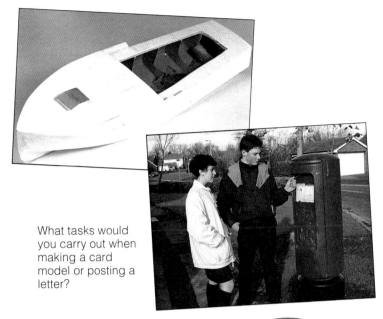

What tasks would you carry out when making a card model or posting a letter?

Activity

▶ What smaller tasks would you carry out if you were:
  (a) making a wooden model
  (b) posting a letter?
  Underline the tasks which you think are most important.

▶ You are organising a disco.
  Across the page are some tasks that you may carry out.
  - Put the tasks in the order that you will do them.
  - Can any tasks be done at the same time if you are working on your own?
  - Can any tasks be done together if someone helps you?

Decorate the room   Book the D.J.   Make the posters

Design the posters   Hire the room   Put up the posters

Buy the food   Print the tickets   Make the buffet

Sell the tickets

Organising a disco. Here are some possible tasks. You may think of others.

When there are many tasks to carry out you must decide how long each will take. It is useful to make a **time plan**.

Activity

▶ You are preparing an evening meal.
  - Decide which type of meal you will make.
  - Decide which tasks you will have to do.
  - Sequence the tasks.
  - Which tasks can be done together?
  - Which tasks have to be done on their own?
  - Decide on a deadline.
  - Write a time plan showing how long each task will take.
  - How can the plan be made more efficient?

EVENING MEAL

Peel potatoes (10 mins)
Wash fish (3 mins)
Grill fish (15 mins)
Weigh frozen peas (2 mins)
Boil water for peas (2 mins)
Boil potatoes (20 mins)
Pour fruit juice (2 mins)
Set table (5 mins)
Slice fruit (10 mins)
Open cream and pour (2 mins)
Simmer peas (5 mins)

A time plan for preparing and making an evening meal

Tick lists

You will be better organised if you write down:
- what you need
- what you have to do.

You can use tick lists to tell you the things you have got and those you still have to get. You can also tick off things when you have done them. The tick list lets you know what you have done and what is still left to do.

Activity

▶ Think of ways in which you could use tick lists:
   (a) at home
   (b) at school
   (c) in business.

▶ Design a tick list for:
   (a) making a meal
   (b) designing a print for a dress or tee-shirt
   (c) a holiday
   (d) making a collapsable deck chair
   (e) carrying out research
   (f) evaluating a design.

Equipment to make a model crane
- Large flat baseboard
- 7 long pieces (15cm)
- 50 short pieces (5cm)
- 1 pulley wheel (25cm diameter)
- 1 winch
- A counterweight
- String
- Glue or rivets
- Dowel to fit pulley wheel
- Hook

Jobs around the house
- Tidy the bedroom
- Make the breakfast
- Brush the dog
- Wash the dinner plates
- Wash and shampoo the car
- Clean shoes

Flow charts

Flow charts are used to show the order in which you carry out tasks. Each task is a short sentence which is boxed or circled. The arrows show the sequence in which the tasks are done.

At the top of any flow chart should be a title that says what is to be done. This is called the **objective.**

Title of activity   Constraints

Get brochure

Choose best trip — Cost?

Contact travel agent — Time available?

Book holiday — Type of travel?

Pay deposit

Activity

▶ What is the objective of the activity opposite?

▶ Make a list of the constraints on each task.

▶ How do these constraints affect how you carry out the task?

▶ Write a new flow chart with the objective of getting to the airport on time.
   Include items such as packing and sorting out tickets.

▶ Write a flow chart for tidying litter in your area or the litter in the photograph opposite.

Storyboards

Storyboards are another way of showing how tasks are to be organised.
Construction kits and DIY manuals often use storyboards to show how to make something.

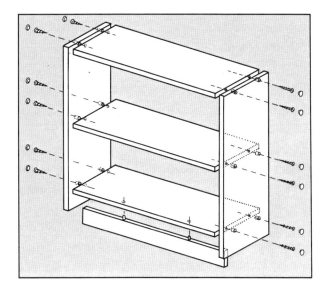

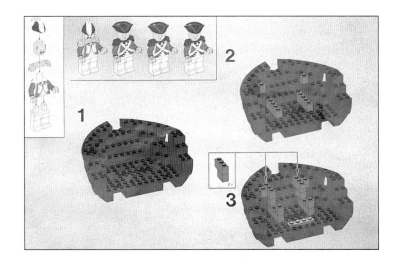

Activity

► What is being constructed in the two photographs here?

► How do the pictures help the person to make the design?

You can use a storyboard to present your designs to an audience. The pictures in the storyboard show how your design developed. Each picture shows the next stage in your design or what happened next.

Activity

► Look at the storyboard below.
  - What is being designed?
  - Write a more detailed description of what is happening in each picture.
  - Design other ways to get people into the water.
  - Draw storyboards to show your design.

► Sketch storyboards to show:
  (a) how to make a sandwich
  (b) how to make a pond

(c) the sequence of events at a set of traffic lights.
You could use a computer graphics program.

► Use storyboards to develop ideas for:
  (a) a system to help the elderly cross roads
  (b) a safe play environment for infants
  (c) the construction of an activity frame for animals.

Working together

You can sometimes become more efficient by organising yourself into teams. You may be able to work with people that have different skills. They can help you. Businesses often work as teams. These include managers and workers. When you are working in a team you must decide:
- who is in charge
- how decisions will be made
- what task each person will do
- how you will pass information to each team member.

Activity

▶ Organise into teams and play the tower building competition.
  - Record all your results.
  - How was your team organised?
  - How well did it operate?
  - Did people work well together?
  - What problems did you have?
  - How might the team work better next time?

THE TOWER BUILDING COMPETITION

- Organise yourself into teams of four.
- Work as a team to build the tallest tower you can with the least materials.
- Decide which tasks each team member will carry out.
- The teacher will supply you with the paper.
- Each group will purchase sheets of paper and tape.
- One sheet of paper costs 1 token.
- One piece of tape costs 1 token.
- The whole task is to be finished in 30 minutes.
- The teacher will award points for height and for stability and completion (maximum 10 marks for each).
- For each token used subtract 1 point.
- The team with the most points wins.

Organising your workspace

You will be able to make your design more efficiently if your work area is tidy and organised. Make sure that you know where everything is. Also make sure that you can find things easily. A badly organised work area could affect how you make your design.

Activity

▶ Look at the old school desk design.
  How would it help a student to be organised?

▶ Compare this desk design to flat desks in your school.

▶ Why are flat desks used today?

▶ Design or re-design:
  (a) a filing system for your records, CDs or toys
  (b) a personal organiser
  (c) a computer desk
  (d) your classroom
  so that you can be more organised.

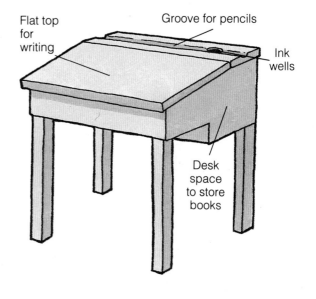

Flat top for writing

Groove for pencils

Ink wells

Desk space to store books

An old school desk design

Costing

Being efficient does not just mean planning and making things on time. It also means making things for the smallest or least cost.

Businesses have many costs:
- hiring or buying the factory
- hiring or buying equipment
- materials to make their products
- wages and salaries of workers
- other costs such as electricity and advertising.

When you make your designs you will need to work out how much they cost. The more materials you use the more the design will cost. Costs will also be high if you use expensive materials and equipment.

A pasta or curry meal

Bedroom artefacts

A pool table

Activity

▶ Make a list of all your costs in a week.
- How can you reduce your costs?
- How will this affect the things you would like to do?

▶ Discuss and list the things you would cost out if you were making the designs in the photographs opposite.

Activity

▶ You are going to design and make a poster for school sports day. Some prices are shown here.
- Decide what materials you will use.
- What other materials might you need?
- Note down the cost of the materials.
- Visit a local shop to see how prices compare.
- How might the poster be made more cheaply?
- How might this affect your design?

▶ When you have decided on your design record all your costs. You could use a spreadsheet to record the costs and work out the total cost of the poster.

▶ Plan to make your poster on a page design computer program. Compare the costs with your plan above.

▶ Carry out your own costing for:
(a) a holiday in the UK
(b) a design to insulate a room against draught
(c) a packed lunch
(d) a 5m x 2m flower bed in a garden.
For each design:
- decide where you will get the information about prices
- decide what the costs will be
- work out the overall cost
- record and present your costs.

SPORTS DAY

A4 paper	£2.15 for 200
Colour photocopy	£6.00
Card	75p for 5
Crayons	£3.05 for 20
Spray mount	£9.50 a can
Sticky labels	79p for 13
Sellotape	89p
Glue	73p
Pritt Stick	89p
Film	£3.99 for 24
Photographs	£2.99 for 24
Letraset	£8.00 a sheet

Materials	Price in shop A	Price in shop B
Paper		
Crayons		

A spreadsheet can be used to record and calculate your costs. A spreadsheet is a grid with headings which you can fill in yourself.

12 DRAWING

Why do we need drawings?

Drawing is very important when designing. You can use drawings to:
- generate ideas for designs
- develop and improve your designs
- present your designs to others
- evaluate your designs.

You should always keep your drawings and sketches. They are useful for looking back at to see how your ideas have developed.

Early ideas for an earring

Activity

▶ Look at the drawings opposite showing how a design developed.
- What is being designed?
- Write a short description of the designs in each picture.
- In what ways do you think the design was improved?

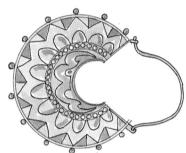

Final ideas for an earring

Concept sketches

Drawings may be very accurate or they may just be rough sketches. By 'doodling' a designer can see what he or she is thinking. These rough sketches are called concept sketches.

Here are some concept sketches for a school mug. They help the designer to generate many different ideas.

Activity

▶ You have been asked to design a mug for your school.
- Draw concept sketches
  You might think about:
  (a) making it easy to hold
  (b) creating a new and unusual range.
- What might be the constraints on your design?

▶ Use concept sketches to develop ideas for one of the following:
(a) a fashion comb
(b) a wall unit to hold books or a TV
(c) a pair of protective oven gloves
(d) a portable telephone
(e) a set of an adventure film
(f) a go-kart.

Concept sketches of a mug

Labelling

Labelling helps to explain what a drawing is all about. If the label gives an explanation as well, the drawing is called an **annotated drawing**.

Remember to keep all labelling brief and to the point.

LOGO
LACE
UPPER
HEEL
TOE
TORSION
SOLE

A labelled drawing

Activity

▶ Use the diagrams across the page to help you design another type of shoe, sandal or slipper.
Annotate your diagrams.

▶ Draw a labelled and annotated diagram of one of the following:
(a) a desk at school
(b) a musical instrument
(c) a piece of electronic equipment
(d) a bath for a disabled person
(e) a tossed salad.

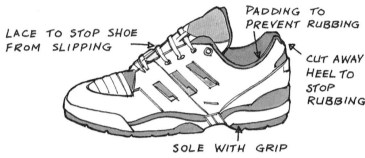

LACE TO STOP SHOE
FROM SLIPPING
PADDING TO
PREVENT RUBBING
CUT AWAY
HEEL TO
STOP
RUBBING
SOLE WITH GRIP

An annotated drawing

Drawing the human body

Sometimes you will need to draw the human body to show your designs. You don't have to draw it exactly. **Pin people** can be used to show:
- clothes and fashion
- how equipment is used
- how people move around a building or in an environment.

Activity

▶ Draw a pin person:
(a) sitting
(b) walking
(c) sleeping
(d) bending
(e) running
(f) climbing.

▶ Add detail to pin people to show ideas for:
(a) clothes for summer or winter
(b) safety clothing and equipment
(c) sports equipment
(d) safety on a vehicle.

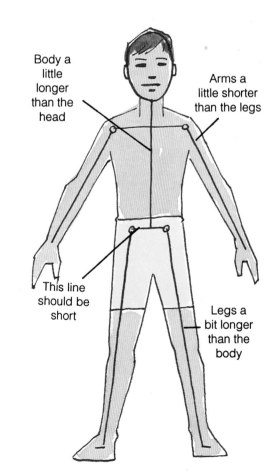

Body a little longer than the head

Arms a little shorter than the legs

This line should be short

Legs a bit longer than the body

Drawing pin people. Draw the pin person first and then add the details.

2D and 3D drawings

Many sketches look flat. We say that flat drawings have **two dimensions** (2D).

To give your picture shape and depth you need to draw it in **three dimensions** (3D). There are different ways to do this. They are shown below.

Activity

▶ Choose any design in the room you are in and draw it in 2D. Choose one method of 3D drawing on this page and draw the design again.

▶ Look at the drawing of the microwave oven. Re-draw it so that the lines do not come to a point in the distance.

▶ Draw one of the following in 3D:
  (a) a video cassette box
  (b) a basket for a pet
  (c) a decorative cake for a party
  (d) a prop for a play
  (e) a hat for a special occasion.

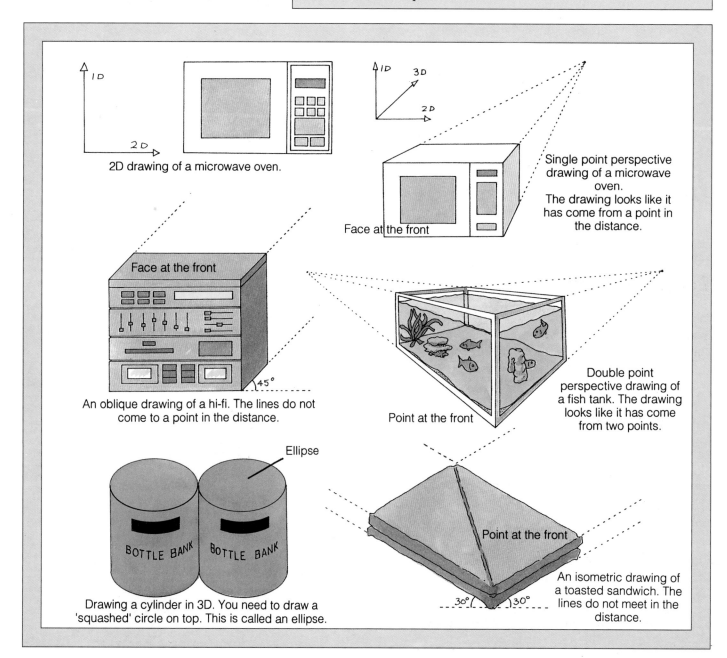

2D drawing of a microwave oven.

Single point perspective drawing of a microwave oven.
The drawing looks like it has come from a point in the distance.

Face at the front

An oblique drawing of a hi-fi. The lines do not come to a point in the distance.

Double point perspective drawing of a fish tank. The drawing looks like it has come from two points.

Point at the front

Ellipse

Drawing a cylinder in 3D. You need to draw a 'squashed' circle on top. This is called an ellipse.

BOTTLE BANK   BOTTLE BANK

Point at the front

An isometric drawing of a toasted sandwich. The lines do not meet in the distance.

Lettering

Lettering can help your drawings. You might write notes on your drawing or write a heading. You must make sure the letters are clear and easy to read. You could try different styles of handwriting or use a stencil.

Computers have very interesting lettering packages. Computer software for word processing and graphics programs often have a variety of lettering. The style of lettering is called a **font**. You can change the size and thickness of the font.

Use construction lines when handwriting and rub them out later

Optima Medium
Gill Extra Bold

Use fonts

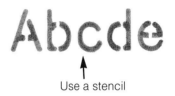

Use a stencil

Activity

▶ Try writing your name in different styles.
  - Use different handwritten styles.
  - Use a stencil.
  - Type your name.
  - Use different fonts on a desktop publishing or graphics program.
  Compare the different methods.

▶ Think of a catch phrase to advertise a product. Design lettering that will make it stand out.

Emphasising

You might want people to notice something on your drawing. You can do this by emphasising it. This means making it stand out.

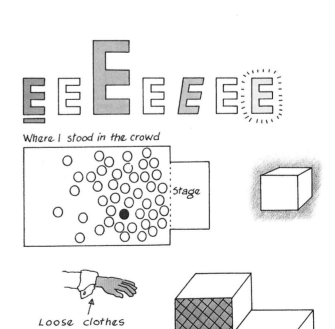

Where I stood in the crowd

Stage

Loose clothes
are dangerous

Activity

▶ How have the items in the pictures been emphasised?

▶ Design ten ways to make your name stand out on a register.

▶ Design a poster about one of the folllowing:
  (a) world famine
  (b) a holiday resort
  (c) safety at work
  (d) a concert/show
  (e) a bargain buy at the shops.
  Use lettering and emphasising in the design.

Shading

When you have finished your 3D drawing it will be a **line drawing**. There will be no shading on it. Imagine a light falling on one side of the drawing. The other sides will be in shadow. You will need to shade them. Drawing a sphere like a tomato or a ball in 3D is quite hard. Shading will help you.

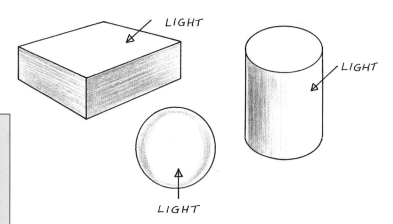

Activity

▶ Draw an apple and a ball with light coming from different directions.
Change the shading on your drawings to show this.

▶ Choose some objects that are cuboids, spheres or cylinders.
Change your shading to make them look:
(a) hollow
(b) solid
(c) textured.

When you are shading, try to follow a straight line. You will not be able to do this on a sphere.

Plans and sections

Many plans are 2D pictures. They usually show a view from above of what the design looks like. Architects' drawings are **plan drawings**.

Imagine cutting through the middle of a design with a knife. What would you see? You can draw what you see as a 2D picture. It shows the details inside. We call this a section. You could also draw a 3D picture.

An architect's plan

Activity

▶ Draw a plan for:
(a) your kitchen at home
(b) a play area for young children
(c) a garden or park
(d) seating at a pop concert or in school assembly.

▶ Draw a 2D or 3D section through:
(a) a piece of food or a meal
(b) a piece of electrical equipment
(c) a torch or plug
(d) an insulated wall
(e) your house.

A section of a cup in 2D and double glazing in 3D

Construction and orthographic drawings

You will need a construction drawing before you make your design. The drawing will show:
- the components or parts of the design
- how you will join together the parts.

Anyone who has bought a model kit or DIY furniture will recognise construction drawings.

Sometimes you need a detailed drawing of your design. You could use an **orthographic projection**. This looks at something in three ways:
- from the front (front elevation)
- from the side (side elevation)
- from the top (plan view).

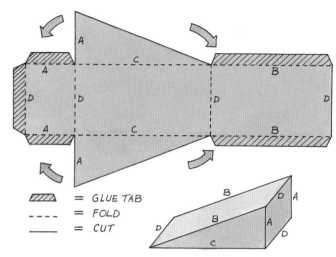

▨▨	= GLUE TAB
- - - -	= FOLD
———	= CUT

Drawing of a model ramp for a wheelchair

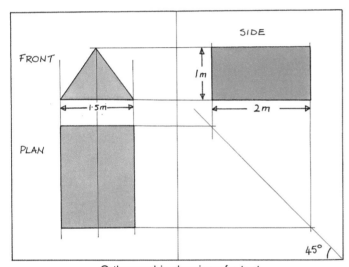

Orthographic drawing of a tent

Activity

▶ Make a construction drawing and an orthographic drawing of an artefact, system or environment.
You could choose designs that use some of these shapes:
(a) a cuboid or rectangular box
(b) a cube
(c) a cylinder
(d) a pyramid
(e) a sphere
(f) an unusual shape such as a milk bottle.

Computer aided design

Computer graphics are used a lot in design work. There are a number of draw and paint software packages available. Designing using computers is called computer aided design (C.A.D.).

Activity

▶ Investigate the paint or draw packages in your school.
- Draw a simple design in 3D using a computer program.
- How does the computer make it easier to draw?
- If you make a mistake, why is it easier to correct on a C.A.D. program compared to a hand drawing?

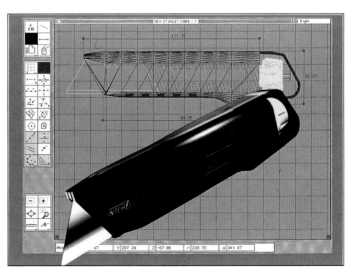

A 3D design of a Stanley Knife drawn and displayed on a computer screen

Why do we model?

Have you ever made something with lego? Have you ever played with a toy doll? These are all models.

Models show designers what the design will look like when it is actually made. The designer will use the model to make sure the design works before it is manufactured properly. A model of a bridge tells a designer if it is safe before it is built. It will also show the designer how well it fits into the environment and how it will help the transport system.

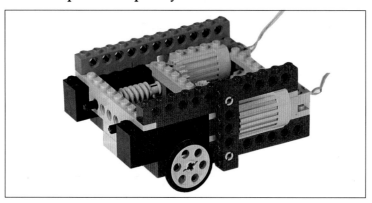

Activity

▶ What is a model?
  Write a short definition.

▶ Why do you think the designs in these two photographs were modelled first before they were made?

Modelling materials

There are many different materials that can be used for modelling. The materials you use will depend on what you are modelling. You would not make a model of a kite out of cement!

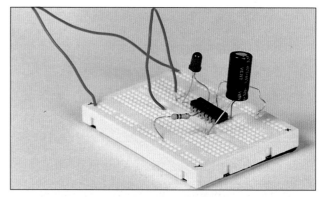

Plastic Card Construction kits
Paper
Tubes   Some modelling materials   Wires
Straws   Polystyrene
Clay   Wood
Pipe cleaners   Plasticine

Activity

▶ Look at the spider diagram showing different materials for modelling.
  Think of a suitable model that could be made with each material.

▶ What materials are used for modelling in the pictures? Why do you think the designer chose these materials?

Scale and proportion

Sometimes models are not the same size as the actual design. They are made to scale. Toys are scale models of real or imaginary things. Each part is made smaller or larger by the same amount so that everything stays in **proportion**.

Cartoons are often drawings where some features are out of proportion. This makes them stand out.

Activity

▶ What is out of proportion in the picture opposite?

▶ Sketch a picture of a friend or object.
Alter the sketch so that certain features are out of proportion.
How could the drawing or a model made from your drawing be useful?

Scaled down models are made smaller and **scaled up** models are made bigger than the actual designs.

Models are scaled down by different amounts. A model of a beach showing pollution might be one thousand times smaller than its actual size. A model of a swing door might be one tenth of its actual size.

Model vehicles

Activity

▶ Look at the photographs of the model vehicles and the ear model.
  - Which of the models is scaled up and which is scaled down?
  - By how much do you think they are scaled up or down (10 times, 100 times or more)?
  - Why might a designer scale down or scale up a model?

▶ In a group, think about a selection of children's toy models.
You might think about your own ideas or look in a catalogue.
Discuss by how much they have been scaled up or down.

▶ Design and make a scale model.
Think about:
  - what you want to make a model of
  - the materials you will use
  - the scale of your model.

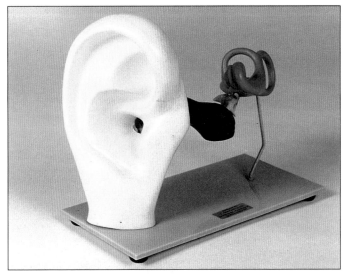

Model of an ear

2D models

Paper and cardboard are good materials for making flat or two dimensional (2D) models. Paper and card can be bent, cut and joined easily.

Activity

▶ What things could you model in 2D?

▶ Design a theatre, a concert stage, or a film set in paper and card.
  - Think about the type of set you are designing and how it will stand up.
  - Will your set be in one or more parts?
  - How will you join the parts?
  - Will they move?
  - Add colour and detail to your model.

▶ Use paper to make model clothes.
  Add colour and detail to your designs.
  What could you use your model to design?

2D model of a concert

Patterns and templates

Patterns and templates are models that are usually made from card or paper. You would use them if you wanted to make lots of the same thing. A template for a size 40 shoe could be used to make thousands of shoes. They would all be exactly the same size.

To make a pattern or template:

Draw the shape of your design onto card or paper

↓

Cut around it, making a 2D shape

↓

Place the pattern or template onto the material you are using and draw around it

↓

The shape is now on the material

↓

Accurately cut around the shape on the material

↓

The pattern or template can be used over and over again

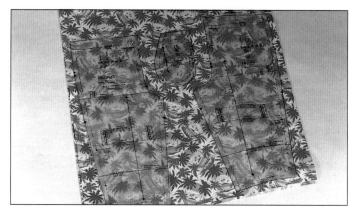

A template used to cut out a fabric pattern

Activity

▶ What things could you make with a template?

▶ Why might you use a template?
  Think about cost, time and waste.

▶ Make a template of your head, hands or feet.
  Use it to make a model of a piece of clothing or footwear.
  You could use a computer software program to draw your template.

▶ Make a template of your body.
  Is it better to make it in one piece or many pieces?
  How could you use this template?

Designs that suit humans

When designing and modelling something you should think about people's size, shape and movement. A child's bicycle is smaller than an adult's. Cupboards are designed so that they open easily and can be reached. Imagine what it would be like trying to saw wood without a handle on the saw!

The study of how things are designed to suit humans is called **ergonomics**. In your designs you should try to:
- make things easier to use
- make things more comfortable or safe
- save space and energy.

How could grips be changed to suit people's needs?

Activity

▶ Look at the drawing at the top of the page. How have the the things been made to suit humans?

▶ Use modelling clay to investigate the grips on pens and keys.
Make models to show how they could be more useful for someone who cannot grip easily.

▶ Use pipe cleaners to make stick people.
Use these to model and investigate the design of:
- seating in a car
- a bike or a motorbike
- a computer work desk.

Our environment is often designed to suit our needs. The layouts of supermarkets and stores are designed to suit shoppers. Our kitchens are designed so that everything is in easy reach.

Activity

▶ How could the layout of supermarket aisles and shop floors help shoppers?

▶ Investigate your bathroom and kitchen. How do designs:
- save space
- reduce the need to bend or lean over?

▶ Use construction kits to investigate:
- space saving in a small kitchen
- improving shop or store design for easy movement
- how to improve your bedroom layout
- how to improve the speed of vehicles.

The layout of shop floors is designed to help shoppers

Pressings and moulds

Modelling clay can be used to take pressings and make moulds of shapes. These can then be used to make models.

You will need to think about how you can use the pressing or mould.

Activity

▶ Make a pressing of your face.
Use the pressing to design a face mask for a cultural or historical play.

▶ Make a pressing of different hand grips.
Use the pressing to design bicycle grips on a sports bicycle.

▶ Make moulds of different fruits.
Use them to design packaging which is secure and does not waste materials.

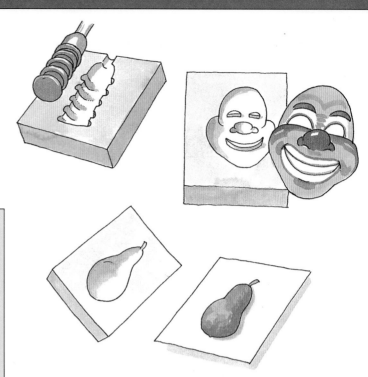

Pressing and moulds for a face mask, a handle grip and fruit

3D models

Three dimensional models are more realistic than 2D models. People will begin to see exactly what your designs look like.

3D models help you to see your ideas from all angles. You will be able to check its:
- size
- shape
- stability.

You can experiment with different materials to make 3D models.

Activity

▶ Use straws or pipe cleaners to make 3D models of furniture.

▶ Use wood or card to make a model of a game or a boat.

▶ Use construction kits to make 3D models of buildings.

▶ Use polystyrene to make 3D models of masks, vehicles or aircrafts.

▶ Use modelling clay to make 3D models of plant pots or crockery.

▶ Use vacuum forming to make 3D models of packaging.

Making a polystyrene model

Vacuum forming to make a 3D model

Mock-ups and prototypes

Models help designers to develop their ideas further. Designers often make:
- mock-ups (a rough model)
- prototypes (a more detailed model)

which can be tested.

They may want to find out:
- whether things fit together
- if they look right
- if they work as expected
- how systems operate
- whether they are the right shape and size.

Mock-ups and prototypes with moving parts are called **working models**.

Activity

▶ What would the designer test on a prototype aircraft wing such as the one in the photograph?

▶ Design a wing with moving parts.
Test your design.
How well does it work?

A prototype of an aircraft wing

Activity

▶ Here are four ideas for mock-ups.
- Choose one model.
- Construct a mock-up.
- Write a few sentences on how your model could be developed.
- Improve the model.
- Test your designs using the model.

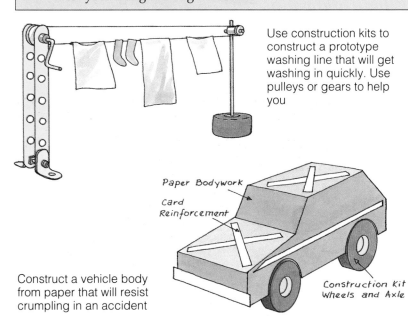

Use construction kits to construct a prototype washing line that will get washing in quickly. Use pulleys or gears to help you

Paper Bodywork

Card Reinforcement

Construction Kit Wheels and Axle

Construct a vehicle body from paper that will resist crumpling in an accident

Construct a mock-up of a system that will reduce long snake-like queues outside sports arenas. Think about how theme parks solve this problem.

Create a mock-up for a pop-up greetings card using paper

Computer aided modelling

Have you ever played a computer game? Have you ever been on a computer simulated ride?

The things you see on the screen in front of you are models. Computers can be used to help you make your models. A 2D model could be a design of a school newspaper page. A 3D model could be of artefacts in a room or a flight simulation.

Activity

▶ Use a computer graphics program to model:
(a) fashion clothing
(b) a layout for an advertising leaflet
(c) a layout for a room.
Experiment with different sizes and colours.

▶ How could your designs be improved?
Use computer models such as simulations and software packages to explore:
(a) people's reaction speeds
(b) environment designs such as energy loss in the home.

A computer aided model

Using computer control you can make robotic models. The computer program will instruct the model to carry out certain tasks. This often means giving instructs for the robot to move.

You can also use a computer program to play music from a keyboard. You can write tunes on the program. It will then play back the music through the keyboard.

Activity

▶ Use a computer program and keyboard to write and play a simple tune.
- Write your tune.
- How can it be improved?
- Try changing the tune and ask for others' opinions.
- Think about how your tune could be used.
- Try changing it to meet the need you have identified.

▶ Design and make a prototype robot system to:
(a) mix food automatically
(b) take messages across a room
(c) move equipment across a desk.
Think about how you would use a motor.
You could write your own computer program.

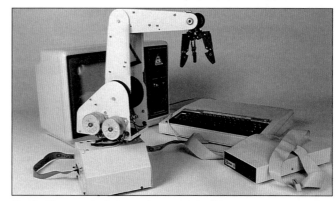
Controlling a robot arm using a computer

Using a music software program

Making models for presentations

Models are very useful for presentations. An audience will be able to see from your model what it is you are trying to make. Your models will often be of new environments.

Architects nearly always make models of the buildings they are designing.

Businesses will make models of new shopping centres.

People trying to show the effect on the environment may make landscape models.

When making models for presentations you should think about:
- what materials you will use
- how you will use colour
- if the model will be in many pieces or in one piece
- what size or scale it will be
- how light or heavy it will be.

Activity

▶ Look at the landscape model across the page.
  - What materials have been used to make it?
  - What scale do you think it is?
  - How do you think the designer could use this model?

Activity

▶ Make a presentation model of one of the following:
  (a) a shopping precinct for a local estate
  (b) the inside of a new water 'fun-centre'
  (c) a layout for a cultural buffet/banquet
  (d) a sports arena
  (e) a golf course
  (f) an adventure playground
  (g) a room in your house showing where cold air gets in.
  The model across the page may help you.

▶ Think of ways in which you would use your model at a presentation.

▶ What needs would your design satisfy?

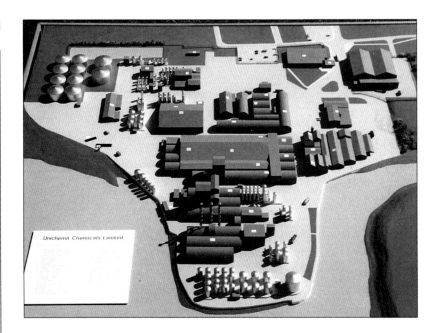

Important terms

Adapting - changing something to suit new needs or situations.

Aesthetics - the appearance of something; its colour, shape, etc.

Alternatives - different possible choices.

Analysis - looking closely at parts of a design specification.

Annotations - notes written on a drawing.

Artefacts - objects that do not usually move.

Assembling - putting pieces together.

Availability - able to get hold of easily.

Brainstorming - coming up with lots of ideas.

C.A.D. - Computer Aided Design.

C.A.M. - Computer Aided Modelling.

Comparing - looking at things which are different about designs.

Components - parts or pieces of a design.

Computer program - a set of instructions which a computer can follow.

Concept sketches - ideas drawn as pictures.

Constraints - limits or restrictions on designs.

Context - where designs are used (home, school, etc.)

Data - facts and figures from research.

Database - lists of facts and figures, sometimes stored on computer.

Degradable - able to decompose or waste away.

Design brief - a short sentence explaining a problem.

Design proposal - writing or drawing showing what is to be made.

Desk top publishing - using a computer to write, draw and print pictures.

Dimensional (2) - something that is flat.

Dimensional (3) - something that has shape and form.

Display - to show off your ideas.

Emphasising - making something stand out.

Environment - our surroundings.

Evaluate - to make a judgement about something.

Finishing - tidying up and removing rough edges.

Flowchart - a chart with step by step ideas or instructions.

Folding - to bend or crease.

Improvising - solving problems in a different way than expected.

Interpreting - deciding what the information is telling you.

Interview - to ask people questions face to face.

Invention - something completely new.

Investigate - to find out by experiment or research.

Isometric drawing - a 3D picture showing lines at the edges.

Joining - fixing things together.

Justifying - giving reasons for your choices.

Labelling - pointing out parts on pictures using words.

Lateral thinking - looking at something from a different point of view.

Manufacture - to make something.

Market research - to find out information from large numbers of people.

Materials - substances used to make designs.

Measuring-up - working out exactly how much material you need.

Mixing - joining different materials together.

Mock-up - a rough model.

Modelling - trying out ideas to see how they will work or look.

Needs - what people want.

Observing - looking at carefully.

Opinion - what you think about something.

Opportunity - a chance to do something.

Orthographic projection - a drawing that looks at a design from the top, side and front.

Pattern - a shape that is followed.

Pattern - information that is linked together.

Plan - an accurate drawing looked at from above in 2D.

Present - to show information or ideas.

Presentation - to talk and show things about a design to an audience.

Prioritise - to put things in order of importance.

Problem - something that needs to be solved.

Proportion - keeping the parts of something to the same scale.

Prototype - an accurate model of a design.

Questionnaire - a list of questions that people fill in.

Record - to write down data.

Refining - improving an idea by changing it a little.

Research - to find out about something.

Review - to look back and reconsider parts of a design or process.

Scale (up) - to make something look bigger.

Scale (down) - to make something look smaller.

Section - a drawing that shows the inside of a design.

Sequencing - placing data in order.

Specifications - the important parts of a design brief.

Spreadsheet - a collection of data and headings, organised in columns and rows, which allows calculations to be made.

Storyboard - a flowchart using pictures.

Survey - to find out what people think.

Symbol - a sign which gives information or instructions.

System - a series of tasks or parts that work together to do a job.

Template - a shape that is placed over material and drawn around before the material is cut.

Testing/trialling - trying out ideas to see if they work.

Timeplan - a list of tasks which must to be done in a certain time.

Word processing program - writing and changing text using a computer.